AGAMEMNON'S KISS

AF751634

INGA CLENDINNEN

was born in 1934. She is a distinguished historian of the Spanish encounters with Aztec and Maya indians of sixteenth-century America, and author of *Reading the Holocaust*, named a *New York Times* best book of the year and awarded the New South Wales Premier's General History Award in 1999. Her 1999 ABC Boyer lectures, *True Stories*, were published in 2000, as was her award-winning memoir, *Tiger's Eye*.

In 2003 *Dancing with Strangers*, her history of the meeting between the original inhabitants of Port Jackson and the British settlers of the First Fleet, was published. The following year it won the Kiriyama Prize for non-fiction, the NSW Premier's Literary Awards (Douglas Stewart Prize for Non-Fiction), the Queensland Premier's Literary Awards (Best History Book) and was shortlisted for the *Age* Book of the Year, the *Courier-Mail* Book of the Year and the Victorian Premier's Literary Award for non-fiction.

{*selected essays*}

agamemnon's kiss

inga clendinnen

text publishing melbourne australia

CONTENTS

The Text Publishing Company
Swann House
22 William Street
Melbourne Victoria 3000
Australia
www.textpublishing.com.au

Copyright © Inga Clendinnen 2006

All rights reserved. Without limiting the rights under copyright above, no part of this publication shall be reproduced, stored in or introduced into a retrieval system, or transmitted in any form or by any means (electronic, mechanical, photocopying, recording or otherwise), without the prior permission of both the copyright owner and the publisher of this book.

First published in 2006 by The Text Publishing Company
This edition 2007

Designed by Chong
Typeset in Granjon by J&M Typesetting
Printed in Australia by Griffin Press

National Library of Australia Cataloguing in Publication data:
Clendinnen, Inga.
Agamemnon's kiss : selected essays.

ISBN 978 1 921145 86 5.

1. Australian essays - 21st century. I. Title.

A824.4

In memory of my unknown donor, April 1994,
and of Helen Daniel 1946–2000

My thanks, as always, to Michael Heyward
and the team at Text

INTRODUCTION

A little over sixteen years ago my old life was ended by severe illness. Four years later I was given a new life through the skill of the Liver Transplant Unit at the Austin Hospital and the kindness of a stranger. For the first weeks after the operation I felt like a hatchling escaped from its tight, white, silent world into this great, vivid, pulsing one. The exhilaration lasted for months. Then I sobered (though not, I'm happy to report, completely) and began, as they say, to consider my position. Clearly my university life was over, and with it the joys of conversations with colleagues, and the incomparable pleasure of guiding intrepid students into the mental worlds of Aztec and Maya Indians. My own explorations into those worlds were also over: my doctors forbad me to return to Mexico. My children were grown and gone. Now my occupation was gone, too.

I think prolonged illness must always do that—put an end to the stories you had been telling yourself about your life. But even while I was still in hospital there had been intimations of a possible new story. Early in my illness I had bought a laptop, in part as talisman from my old life, in part to fill the empty days. I wrote about the horizontal people around me, and some of the vertical ones too; about the memories that came drifting from childhood in the silence of the night and stayed to haunt my days. A woman named Helen Daniel who had reviewed my book on the Aztecs came to visit me, became my friend, and chivvied me into writing more (I tell something of this in the essay called 'Backstage at the Republic of Letters'). Helen didn't seem to care what I wrote so long as I kept writing, which is a long way from academe. So I wrote a very short story about strangers on a train and a longer one about a sour old woman; they won prizes; I was back in the turning world again. Another woman who knew my Mexican work asked me to write something for a collection of essays she was putting together: I wrote 'About Bones'. My new life had begun before I knew it.

Since then I have written four books: *Tiger's Eye*, which recorded what it feels like to fall into the underworld of sickness and then to clamber out again, one on the Holocaust to exorcise some of its horror by steady looking, and two on the relations between sea-voyaging British and land-voyaging Australians from their first meeting in 1788. If I had not fallen ill I would have written none of them. I also wrote essays, some in parallel with the books, some at tangents from them, and some about the accidental collision between a particular thought and a particular moment in time.

I like writing essays because they are short, as I now know life is. They are also about the right length for the way we live now: for reading in waiting rooms, between planes, on planes; for putting yourself to sleep at night; for thinking about when you can't sleep. But it is only now that I have been instructed to write this introduction that I begin to wonder what these things called 'essays' are. My dictionary is not much help. It tells me that 'essay. n.' means 'Attempt (at); a literary composition (usu. prose & short) on whatever subject'; and that 'essay, v. t.' means to 'try, test (person, thing), to attempt'. These things piled in front of me are short, they are certainly not poetry, they are on a bewildering array of subjects. They are also, heaven knows, 'attempts'. They do not look like 'finished work' at all. Sometimes they end with a question mark. But what else are they?

The odd thing is that I know what essays are not. I know you can't preach in an essay because it turns into a sermon; you can't teach in an essay because it turns into a lecture; you can't exhort in an essay because it turns into a harangue, and you can't dredge the mud at the bottom of your soul because then it will turn into a confession. In the dry-mouthed panic of a radio interview I once said that essays were like love affairs, meaning they were intimate, brought unexpected pleasure and usually didn't last very long. Now I realise they are nothing like as intense as a love affair, and that that is their quality. Nothing much hangs on them beyond the pleasure we take in them. A friend suggested they were like eighteenth-century letters: a pleasurable, elegant pastime for a rainy afternoon. It's true that eighteenth-century letters were not 'private'. The letter-writers knew their letters were likely to be read aloud before a family or some larger company. But by the nineteenth-century letters had lost that public dimension, and that creates a problem. Chekhov and Flaubert wrote many letters, but they would never have consented to our reading them. For one thing, they were artists. (Flaubert could spend a whole day on a sentence. We know that from a letter.) They would not want us to see them in a state of literary undress. More important, their letters are hand-crafted for a particular recipient. To his brother Chekhov writes gaily and tenderly; to his accountant wittily and sometimes crossly. Embarked on his Egyptian adventure Flaubert writes to his mother (he calls her 'Darling', and means it) swearing he is keeping himself healthy, warm, clean and well-rested. Meanwhile he is boasting to a friend left sulking in Rouen of his lascivious exploits with the local whores, especially 'the famous courtesan' Kuchuk Hanem. He also remarks that he has picked up yet another dose of the clap.

Reading letters addressed to other people might be endlessly beguiling, but it is a shabby thing to do. Our punishment for it is watching all that affection, all that verve and wit, flowing to some other person, and knowing it will never, never be directed to us.

Diaries, then? When Virginia Woolf was trying to pin down the peculiar charm of Samuel Pepys' diary she decided it was because Pepys, being in public life a great and powerful civil servant—the Father of the Modern British Navy, no less—and unable to unbend in public, chose instead to unbend to us: 'The Diary runs naturally from affairs of State and the characters of Ministers to affairs of the heart and the characters of servant girls; it includes the buying of clothes, the losing of tempers, and all the infinite curiosities, amusements, and pettinesses of average human life.' Woolf is guiltily glad that Mrs Pepys was a less-than-perfect confidante: 'otherwise she would have enjoyed the confidences we now enjoy.'

So. Woolf thinks this is pillow-talk we are listening to. I don't. The diary, or most of it, is in cipher. Do you write pillow-talk in cipher? I think it was intended not only to be private, but to stay private. True, it is expansive: Pepys records where he goes, whom he meets, what he eats. He drinks too much, swears he'll not drink for a week, doesn't; he has a cold, 'a spoonful of honey and a nutmeg scraped into it did me much good'. He is in raptures over the spread his new maid contrives for what he describes as a small family dinner: 'We had a fricassee of rabbits and chickens, a leg of mutton boiled, three carps in a dish, a great dish of a side of lamb, a dish of roasted pigeons, a dish of four lobsters, three tarts, a lamprey pie (a most rare pie), a dish of anchovies, good wine of several sorts, and all things mighty noble and to my great content.' We are happy for him while we worry about the spread of his girth and the state of his heart. He loses his dog on a river excursion with his wife; they search for it; they find it and rejoice; we are glad he likes his dog. He likes his wife, too, and enjoys her company, but that does not mean he is faithful to her. He frets about his mother, who is more irritable every day, about trouble in the office, about a naval captain who contemplates suicide but decides to turn Quaker instead. He arranges a pension for his father, and manages to shift the cost onto his brother. He practises the conventional social deceptions, and resents the necessity: 'Went to hear Mrs Turner's daughter play on the harpsichord...it was enough to make any man sick to hear her [but] I was forced to commend her highly.' He even records the delicate venalities that oil the creaking Stuart bureaucracy: 'Going out of White Hall, I met Captain Grove, who did give me a letter directed to myself from himself. I discerned money to be in it, and took it, knowing, as I found it to be, the proceed of the place I have got him...I did not open it till I came home, and there I broke it open, not looking into it till all the money was out, that I might say I saw no money in the paper, if ever I should be questioned about it'; we shake our heads and think '*Plus ça change*.'

The charm of the diary is precisely that we should not be hearing any of this. We are eavesdropping on the conversation Samuel Pepys is conducting with himself in the privacy of his own head. I think his daily diary is this lively, unreflective man's attempt to keep track of himself and of his life through the surge and whirl of experience. Did he ever go back to read it? I doubt it. I think the business of taming the day into a secret cipher was enough to satisfy his need to order his frenetically busy, multi-level life. If it did not sound anachronistic, I would say that Pepys' diary was therapeutic.

It is also, of course, delectable gossip, made doubly delectable because this gossip comes out of the mouth of the star witness/performer. But our pleasure is reprehensible and we know it, because Pepys believes he is talking only to himself. He would be chagrined to think we are still mulling over his feelings for his dog, his passion for roast protein, his practised duplicities.

By contrast, Michel de Montaigne, Seigneur of Eyquem and

acknowledged Father of the Essay, is always ready for conversation. It is true he is not much interested in gossip. While he enjoys the spectacle of social foolishness, his main interest is in anatomising it the better to understand humanity. In that great pursuit he is ready to investigate anything and to go anywhere, including his own dwindling interest in and capacity for lust. He uses himself as his primary subject not through vanity or any desire to impress, but because, as he says jauntily, 'I have no other business but myself', and so is always available for examination. Gossip sickens where there is so much candour.

It is hard to explain what makes his essays so enchanting, but I think it is the lithe, athletic movement of a naturally intrepid mind. He talks about anything because he is afraid of nothing, and he keeps talking because he is always curious and never satisfied: 'I am seeking the truth, not laying it down.' His moral force comes from that mobile, fearless intelligence. He often talks about injustices (never 'injustice' in the abstract. Montaigne is always particular) but he wants us to think about them, not to do anything about them, or at least not right now. That is his invitation into every subject: to think about it, to search out its meanings—to share his surprise or joy or horror that there are such things in this green world.

He is ruthlessly honest, especially with himself. Most of us want to claim the melancholy that comes with the years to be 'wisdom', or if not quite wisdom, 'maturity'. Montaigne began writing his essays when he was 38. He was still writing them when he died 21 years later, but he resolutely refuses to admit any improvement: 'My first edition dates from 1580: I have long since grown old but not one inch wiser. "I" now and "I" then are certainly twain, but which "I" was the better?'

Michel de Montaigne, Father of the Essay, is not talking to his diary or his pillow or his God: he is talking directly, happily, to us. He is unpredictable in everything except in his intelligence, the economy and grace of his language, and the comfortable good humour of his relationship with his readers. I have come to think that it is this power to establish affectionate trust—to assume liberty, equality and fraternity between reader and writer—which marks out the essay from all other forms of written communication.

So now, rather too late, I think I know what an essay is: a direct, equal, personal communication on a matter of shared interest between writer and reader. I hope the pieces of writing that follow are essays, though some were first written as lectures and others as book reviews. I have made a few stylistic revisions and deleted the footnotes but I haven't tried to update them because essays belong to the moment.

The first section, 'Backstage', is largely about things I have thought and felt; the second, 'Dispatches', about public things that have engaged my attention; the third, 'Secret Lives', about the mysterious communion between writer and reader and about some of the writers who have brought me special joy. The final essay, 'Agamemnon's Kiss', is my attempt to explain to you and also to myself why, after fifty years, I still find the doing of history addictive. But I know that when I am weary of the world's commotion, and even of history, I will find time to visit my friend Michel de Montaigne. I will tap on his library door; he will look up from his desk, lay down his pen and say, 'Welcome! I've just been thinking about Coaches.' Or Cannibals. Or The Art of Conversation. And he will begin to talk.

As I write this I realise that my friend Montaigne has taught me one large thing among a cloud of small, delightful ones. It took some time for me to understand that this cheerful, sanguine man's central preoccupation is with death and how we ought to meet it. Ought we rehearse it? Or ignore it? Ought we outwit it by choosing the moment of our exit? Montaigne circles the subject, stalks it, draws back from it, reflects on it. Then he decides, expressing his opinion with his customary élan: 'Let death take me as I am planting my cabbages, indifferent to him, and still less that my garden is still not finished.' This declaration of terminal insouciance is followed immediately by a joke: 'I saw one [man] die, who at his last gasp, complained of nothing so much as that destiny was about to cut the thread of a chronicle history he was then compiling, when he had got no further than the fifteenth or sixteenth of our kings.' And there we are, four hundred years later, laughing with Montaigne at the spectre standing snubbed in the cabbage-patch, and the lovely absurdity of men.

Now I know how I want death to come for me: not in my cabbage patch, but strolling in the slanting rain of light through eucalyptus leaves, a strip of bark in my fingers, the gurgle of hidden magpies all around. I will say to Death 'A moment, friend.' And then: 'I'm ready now.'

I BACKSTAGE

BIG LOUIS

Big Louis is dead. I found out only yesterday, because the last time I went to the clinic I didn't meet any of the people who might have told me, which can happen when you're down to three-monthly visits. He might have died as long as five months ago. It is odd to discover you have been orphaned for months without knowing it. Louis was the first person to receive a liver transplant at the unit when it started at the Austin Hospital here in Melbourne in 1988. Units were already working in Brisbane and Adelaide, but he was our first. They'd tried transplanting livers long before that but everybody used to die, so they gave up for a while, but in the early eighties they began again. What had changed the odds were better operating techniques and yet another miracle drug, this one called Cyclosporin. Cyclosporin controlled rejection without too much damaging the patient. It came into use only in 1989, so Louis must have survived his first few months without it. The unit people must have been proud of him.

So Louis was Number One. The last one, operated on about a week ago, is Number 301. I am Number 108, from April 1994. We write our history in the old-fashioned way here. Dates and numbers matter in this long, thin, accidental family I have joined. We care about lines of descent, too, so Louis was our grandfather. He was a big, slow-moving Frenchman or Belgian in his late sixties who couldn't or wouldn't speak English. He would sit peaceably in the waiting room on his too-small chair, one large hand on each knee, and exude the mild benignity of an elephant, or perhaps a bishop. It was good to see him slowly moving up the corridor ahead or lying back in the padded chair for the routine blood test. He was our talisman against the fates, and we took comfort from his being.

My new family has no politics, and prior relationships are erased on entry. Class is erased too. Because humans happen to be endowed with two kidneys and only one is necessary for life, a friend or kinsman might surrender the other to a specified donor, as Kerry Packer's helicopter pilot recently did in a blare of ambiguous publicity, but even our richest man couldn't buy himself a liver. 'Living cadaver' transplants, as they are called—liver, heart, lungs—are done democratically, in designated public hospitals, with public patients queued in accordance with need. We are nonetheless selective. There are no honorary members. The only way into the family is by way of the operation. People on the waiting list don't even meet us post-transplant people, except for a single person selected by the unit to be their counsellor or 'next friend'. This segregation might be no more than a way of ordering the doctors' time, with some days being allocated to a string of individual pre-transplant interviews and some to the crush of the post-transplant clinics with people being called into the offices one by one, but I suspect it is also policy. People on the waiting list panic easily. They need to know some things, but not others, and they haven't yet learnt to trust the medicos, who naturally want to control the information flow so that no one gets muddled or demoralised. But we sometimes meet. Before my transplant I had just seen my doctor and was waiting by the unit's lift, shaking, yellow, cradling my distended belly with my arms (advanced liver disease swells the abdomen grotesquely) when a slender sari-wrapped Indian lady was suddenly beside me, holding my shaking hands in her steady warm ones and saying 'You'll be all right. I promise you, you will be all right. It is only three months for me and look, already so well!' She smiled into my eyes like a loving little sister. 'And today I am off to Sydney to be with my husband! They are letting me go to Sydney!' The lift doors opened, she pulled my head down and kissed me firmly on the forehead, pushed me inside, and I saw her blessing me through the closing crack as I slid through the floor.

I was startled by this emotional surge from a delicately scented stranger, but I was also warmed by it. Months later, after my own transplant, I felt the same surge of affection for a yellow, wasted man also trying to cradle his swollen belly, and in exactly the same place: the little hall by the lift outside the Liver Transplant Unit's offices. I shared her impulse but lacked her courage. I didn't speak. Guilt lived with me until I came across the man in the surgical ward after his transplant, transformed back to his original form of a small tough Scot with a spiky ginger moustache, and cheerfully remembering 'the little Asian-looking fella' he had once been.

A handful of pre-transplant people are terrified or suspicious or downright paranoid about the whole business, which can seem surreal, and then someone who has been through it is allocated to them to calm them. One woman I was sent to see sat huddled in a blanket in her hospital bed, persuaded that the doctors had not the least concern for her welfare and were intent on experimenting on her body. Another, startlingly beautiful even in her flattened state, was incandescent with rage at the unseemly eruption of the physical melodrama that had plucked her from the world and sequestered her in a tiny blue-curtained tent (she kept her bed curtains furiously drawn). She had festooned the tent with what looked to be hundreds of cards: communiqués from her lost life. She finally agreed to the transplant, I think largely because I described the process of the alternative death in some detail. Then she died anyway. Most people on the waiting list die. Australia has a very low donor rate, one of the lowest in the world, which used to surprise me. I thought a bunch of secular humanist hedonists like us would be easy givers, and suspected the influx of migrant families with strong religious backgrounds explained the low rate. But that is not the case. Provided the correct rituals are followed (naked candles in Intensive Care if required), those families tend to be generous. Perhaps the hedonism is the problem. Perhaps we refuse to think about death exactly because we do believe it is the end, so there can be no previous discussion because everyone has decided they will live forever. And families lurching under the brutal impact of grief are asked to allow a loved one's body to be, as they think of it, pillaged. That is why the recent scandals in Britain about the unauthorised taking of organs for research distress me. They will make people even less ready to think about the simple realities, so even more people will die.

For we lucky few who enter the family, the bencfits are multiple. For example: the worst thing about being seriously ill is the loneliness. You know that nobody, neither your doctor nor your husband nor your best friend, can imagine what it feels like, especially in its more trivial manifestation: how your left calf will clench and tremble for no reason, how dread comes sliding smoothly out from behind the water jug. Your new family knows. They will say: 'It was my right leg used to do that, quiver like a mad thing. And in the small of your back, like a big vibrator buried in your spine, do you get that?' and you say, with relief, 'Yes I do,' and the loneliness is less lonely, and you know there will be someone ready to listen when you need to talk about fluttering muscles, inexplicable tastes in the mouth, inexplicable tears. The doctors might give you a brisk explanation as to the why of it, but they can't help you find the words to describe how it feels.

In the clinic I also found again the radiantly chaotic social world I thought I had lost when I left primary school and began a lifetime of picking and choosing friends and associates. The studious egalitarianism of the Australian national health system serves up a marvellous mix of genders, ages, classes and ethnic origins. As it turns out—as my betters have told me but I had never really learned—the greatest of these is class. People I would never have met, never glanced at, never even seen in my ordinary life as a middle-class academic of Anglo ancestry were now sitting next to me for a couple or more hours at a time as we waited our turn with the doctor. I had the privilege of coming to know, for example, Gloria. She had to be up by 4.30 a.m. on Clinic days to come in to Clinic by public transport from her distant outer suburb: a place where I had never been, whose name was no more than a sociological tag for deprivation and disorder. She didn't really have to leave so early, but she dreaded being late for Clinic and seeming less than grateful. She would be home again by mid-afternoon, to deal with her two small children and her superbly unco-operative husband. The drugs had happened to work in her to produce a soft flow of surplus flesh. Most of us had had our adventures with our protean bodies, but no one else billowed with flesh as Gloria did. She had also become chronically breathless and uncertain of her balance, and now she was diabetic, which sometimes happens. You can't fool with bodies without some unintended consequences. Gloria would sit with her pretty hands in her matron's lap and the face of a pretty girl lost somewhere in her wide one, and when she saw me she would direct a vague smile somewhere past my right shoulder and pat the seat she had been keeping beside her. As far as I could discover (she spoke little and softly) she was at once desperately shy, shamed by her shyness, and shamed by her flesh. She was also determined to be stoical, which is why she needed a friendly presence beside her. Some husbands and wives always came to the clinic with their spouses to act as talking chiefs for them, thereby re-enacting a way of being married I had forgotten about. Gloria had to get through everything alone. She was fiercely grateful to the unit's doctors, and fiercely obedient to their instructions. We all were—we knew what we owed them—but we would moan and groan and trade jokes about them. Gloria never did. These people had chosen her, and cared for her, as I think no one had done before.

Pat wasn't shy, just scary. He looked as if he had been rough-carved over a chunk end of redgum; a long bristle of red hair ran right down the middle of his big bare skull; and his arms, and for all we knew all of him, were blue with tattoos, most of an embarrassingly intimate nature. No one was game to talk to him, but I thought he could scarcely turn on a grey-haired old granny, or not in the unit's waiting room, and one day I sat next to him. He had been, as he looked and in his own description, 'a very bad lad', deeply into illegal substances, violence, motorbikes and alcohol. Then at twenty-eight he discovered he had ruined his liver and that he might well die soon and unpleasantly, and immediately after that some well-spoken strangers in white coats were ready to try to give him another chance provided he mended his ways. So he did. He gave up drink, drugs, even smoking, and now when he went to the pub to see his mates he drank lemon squash. He'd also sold his motorbike. If he wanted to go anywhere he walked or rode his push-bike or took a train. (He lived in a suburb where train travel was quite peaceful, provided you were built like a tree.) He was translucently proud that his thirteen-year-old son was building his first motorbike in the garage—he'd done the same when he was thirteen—but he himself was through with them. They were too dangerous, now that his body didn't belong exclusively to him. He had tried to throw his life away, and it had been given back to him. He would not throw it away again. What was most remarkable about Pat—what I privately thought rare and noble about him—was his refusal to moralise from his experience. He was utterly free from the middle-class urge to preach. This had been his personal lesson, and he had learnt from it. He's still going well.

Most arguments against transplants make me angry, like those made by fastidious people who do not suffer from a terminal disease and who find the notion of brain death too complicated or the whole idea of transplantation of organs too aesthetically distasteful to be contemplated, when all the while here we are in our various bodies, walking around enjoying ourselves. We are the argument for it. Of course our situation is a touch precarious. Given the chronic shortage of donors, what being accepted on to the waiting list for a transplant most feels like is being snatched out of a turbulent river and hoisted up onto a rickety suspension bridge. You know you would have died in the water, but you still don't feel too safe. But soon the people ahead of you on the bridge are turning to hug you, cheering you on, telling you the quivering and rocking is normal, the vertigo is normal, everything is normal, that you will be, indeed you already are, fine. Over the next few weeks or months you meet more of your new family, and sooner or later they'll point to a slow-moving shape up ahead, and say, 'That's Louis. He's Number One.' And now Louis is gone we turn and clutch each other, because without his weight the bridge is trembling.

2001

BACKSTAGE AT THE REPUBLIC OF LETTERS

(Note: this began life as a lecture, and it shows.)

Why do we think that reading is good for humans? Its survival value would seem negligible, even negative. When we are reading we are not usefully employed killing something, we are not making anything, we're not even being sensibly cautious. Tigers could sneak up on us while we sit deaf and blind, head down, at the cave entrance. So what's the use of it? To assess that, I will follow the time-honoured investigative strategy of the Humanities of taking myself as subject to assess grander issues.

First, an outline of my recruitment into what I think of as the secret society of readers. I grew up in what a linguist would call 'an impoverished oral culture with a severely limited speech-code': a lower-middle-class household in a provincial Australian town where the only acknowledged moral and intellectual aspiration was how to achieve respectable reproduction. Speech acts were emphatically instrumental: 'do the dishes, feed the dog, stop that, keep quiet, go away'.

While anthropologists would classify it as an oral culture, it was in actuality a largely silent one. The only voices I could rely on hearing were on the radio: the ABC, which would be left on all day by my hard-pressed mother until the men came home in the evening. There was an unforeseen and emphatically undesired consequence. Those were carefully spoken days (it was rumoured that ABC announcers donned dinner suits to read the news) so when I at last began to talk I spoke with much the same plummy accent and intonation as I do today, to the chagrin and enduring humiliation of my family. (If I did some research and listened to the ABC archives from about 1936 to 1938, I'd probably find the parents of my voice.)

In my house I wasn't read to. If my father were home and sitting down he would be asleep, and I don't think my mother sat down at all. Life was hard on women back then. I put off talking until I was three or so, scuttling around silently while my aunts nobly strove to keep their conviction that I was backward from my mother, and failing on average three times a week. I wasn't backward. I was simply beginning to dread that what I saw might be exactly what I was going to get.

It was about then that I had my first experience of the book as instrument of oppression. It was, as most things seem to turn out to be, my mother's fault. She told me that a little sprite or elf (its exact ontological status was obscure) lived behind the ventilator grille in the kitchen—you know the ventilators in those old weatherboard houses—and this elf had two books, one golden, one black. He would watch through the ventilator, and when you did a good deed he would write it down in his golden book, and when you did a bad one he would write it in the black book. For a while all my mother needed to do if I was engaging in some illicit activity was to flick her eyes up to the grille; I'd look too and think I'd seen a flash of movement, as you do; and desist. I did notice he was never around when I was executing a good deed, which didn't happen often, but did happen.

I came to hate that elf. For a while I tried going into the dining room to escape the spy in the ventilator, until I realised there was a ventilator in there too; that he could probably sneak all over the house. For a while I retreated under the dining room table to perform any serious acts of mischief, but my mother soon twigged to that.

And then I had a liberating insight. So this character kept his black book and his golden book. So what? What was it to me? I came out from under the table, performed my evil acts at will, saying, inwardly: 'Scribble on, creep!' It was an early and permanently persuasive lesson that at base all religion is a method of social control. It was also a disturbing preliterate discovery: these things called books could be used for evil purposes.

Soon after that the tribe of giants who ran the place decided to teach me to read, and when I was about eight they finally succeeded. Once I'd got the knack of it I couldn't believe that reading was legal, because (while I didn't yet know the word) the whole enterprise was so subversive. The tall lady behind the tall desk at the Geelong Public Library would stamp anything I took up to her—there didn't seem to be children's books in those days—and I'd be out the doors, down the stairs, onto the tram and home free. With the books. It was as if this whole massive edifice I had thought so solid was riddled with tiny burrows like a Swiss cheese, and in each burrow was a book, and in each book was a voice ready and eager to talk to me, at length and about anything. I discovered there were books at home, a whole dark shelf of them stowed away in the hall cupboard. There was a Bible inscribed by the minister who officiated at my parents' marriage, which I read with stunned attentiveness, a volume of Shakespeare's Tragedies (another implausible wedding present?) and half a dozen or more small red volumes which had been my mother's school prizes dating from the first decade of the century just passed. They were mainly nineteenth-century British novels, I suppose because they were classics and thought to be uplifting, but Smollett had somehow got in there too. (There's a legacy: I don't really like large, beautifully-produced hardbacks. My taste runs to small books with muddy print on stuff like blotting paper, with the dye on the cover coming off on your hands, like Lady Macbeth.)

Between library and home I became a passionate reader, which took me out of my depressed social class and to the University, which was free and open to passionate readers in those far-off days, and there I wallowed in the joys of promiscuous reading, as I wallow still.

There are legacies from those secret childhood experiences. For example, I worry about children these days. I hear them sunnily discussing the last Children's Book Award list with the Children's Librarian, I watch them coming out of the libraries with their arms stacked high with their week's reading, and I worry: how will they cope with the rigours of solitary grown-up reading after all these lucid, friendly books, eager to please as puppies? Where is the murk? Where are the intoxicating mysteries? Why does Macbeth call himself by that list of different names? Did Lady Macbeth see Banquo's ghost and pretend she didn't or couldn't she see it at all; was the ghost there or wasn't it; what difference would that make anyway? Troubling—and intoxicating. (Let me say for my nine-year-old's money, and possibly still, *Macbeth* beats the other plays hands down.)

There is another legacy: my aversion to polemical writing. The aversion is partly pragmatic: when did you last change your mind because you were yelled at? It is partly principled: as a practising democrat I think people have both the capacity and the right to make up their own minds, especially on important matters. But now I realise it goes further back. It springs from my childhood notion of books as burrows with fine things at the end of them. I spot a promising burrow, I slither hopefully down—and there is this fellow (it usually is a fellow) wagging his finger and ranting at me, and I fall over backwards getting out of there. Of course there are some intricate and deep-branching burrows like the ones I've been re-exploring lately called *The Making of the English Working Class*, or *Gulliver's Travels*, written with passion, and from which you emerge changed; but they are designed to beckon you further and deeper while giving you at least the illusion of choosing your own way. There is no finger-wagging at all.

My next experience of literacy-as-liberation came from the experience of teaching, first at the University of Melbourne, later at the new University of La Trobe. I've always been sceptical of people who claim to have been around during a golden age, but the seventies and eighties at La Trobe still look golden to me: a young, eager staff and a marvellous mix of students of all ages and classes and ethnic backgrounds, most of them the first of their family to be at the university, and therefore with no idea what it was reasonable to ask of them. And all of us revelling in the new pleasure of reading about knotty matters in private, then discussing those matters with ten or twelve other people in a classroom over three hours; then reading more, and meeting again, talking again...Golden days.

Then came Dawkins and the Age of Iron, in which we now live. As teaching conditions deteriorated I used illness as an ejector seat to escape from academe and into the independence of full-time writing.

I had begun to write, or to try to, as my children grew older and because I knew I should, but at first I had been paralysed because I could only imagine my potential audience as a handful of scowling academics. Then suddenly I began to write quite tough, specialist history, deciphering documents, reconstructing episodes, with no anxiety about audience at all. Why? Because I realised I already knew them. They were my students, or kin to them. There they were, still shaking their heads, refusing to dance to my tune, even trying out steps of their own, but now on the other side of the page instead of the table. So for my wider audience I simply did the same things I used to do with my students: laying out the issues, telling them why I thought they were worth thinking about, introducing and evaluating the sources, then leading what were now my fellow investigators through different analytic procedures, testing the usefulness and the limitations of each one as we went; and at the end summing up how far we had got, how far we still had to go, and what sources and analytic techniques might get us there. However exciting the texts, the core narrative was always the process of the inquiry.

The die was cast: I would write serious history, but I would not write for the eight other experts in the field. I would not take it as my duty to rehearse the historiography, or to advance the particular discussions dominating the field at the time. Instead I would write in the hope of seducing an intelligent, non-specialist audience into giving me a large slice of their uncommitted time: into thinking about the issues I most cared about, perhaps into reading more about them, perhaps even going back to the texts themselves.

I could do that because history is a democratic discipline. We have no esoteric skills, although we might pick up some peculiar habits, like deciphering ancient inscriptions or reading Nahuatl, along the way. We have no esoteric language, despite occasional attempts to invent one. We have to live with the fact that ordinary people are practising historians too. They have to be, to manage in the world. They have to learn to assess the plausibility of the stories other people spin to them; to reflect on motives overt, covert or hidden even from the tellers. They have to make decisions about what they will do next, based on their analysis of past experience. And enough of them are deeply curious about other people, including people who live differently from them, if they think there's a fighting chance of finding out something authentic about them.

Academic historians' only professional advantage is that we have the time and the accumulated experience to guide the amateurs.

From my own experience I'd say that guidance does not mean simplification. There may be an issue in source criticism or a dispute over word-meanings best relegated to a footnote, or even to a scholarly article. But time and again I've been tempted to slide over something difficult, to make something look simple when it was not; I resisted the temptation; and time and again readers have demonstrated that I was right to do so. I now think my readers are as enthralled by the tough issues as I am—provided the expression of the difficulties is as clear as I can make it. 'Popular' history need not mean—must not mean—dumbed-down history.

When I was asked to do the Boyer Lectures for the ABC, friend of my youth, I had to make a sudden dive into Australian history, which I enjoyed, but giving the lectures was a seriously weird experience: sitting alone in a tiny room, reading out words I'd written while sitting alone in a rather larger room, hoping but not believing that somewhere out there somebody—anybody—was listening. I was made to realise how dependent I was, when writing, on imagining audience response; that for me writing was a kind of (admittedly one-sided) conversation.

Then I wrote *Tiger's Eye*, or rather wrote the words which became *Tiger's Eye*. I had written those words to hold my self together through difficult times. It was not an act of communication but, if you like, of private therapy: a continuing demonstration of the power of writing to focus and steady consciousness and so to maintain the continuity of one's being. I then discovered that 'reader response' was much more protean, much more explosive, than I had thought. For the first time I met some of the people who had sat silent and alone reading the words I had written as I sat silent and alone—and received a fast and bruising education in reception theory.

I realised that through all those earlier years I had been imagining a pre-trained audience: one that shared my academy-based expectations as to what was going on on the page. You notice that even on occasions like this, when we are meeting face to face, we talk within the conventions in which we write. We complain when a writer's conventions don't fully mesh with ours, which is one reason why we give renegade academic popularisers such a hard time, and if we have a dispute over meaning we typically rush back to scrutinise the text.

But even academics are sometimes brought to acknowledge that we do not control how our work will be read, as when it goes into translation. A book of mine went into Spanish, Italian, Portuguese. Fine. It still looked like the same book. I could even read bits of it. Then one went into Polish and into Hebrew. Well...that was okay. They were unintelligible to me, but they were European languages. Sort of. Then *Aztecs* was translated into Mandarin, and I felt deeply queasy. I knew it wasn't likely—but what would happen if a billion Chinese read my *Aztecs*? I had no idea, and I did not want to take responsibility.

So...while the audience response to *Tiger's Eye* was thrilling, it was also scary. People read it as their individual experience dictated: as a book about childhood, or about being ill or about dying; about family, about dealing with mothers. I did not want to take responsibility for what reading it led some people to do. For example: one woman wrote to tell me she had made up a list of questions she was taking to her obdurately reticent mother, who happened to be on her death bed at the time, and that this time, she intended to get some answers.

I discovered from all that that books do make things happen, but not always what you had in mind; that reading is a creative activity, and most creative, I suspect, for people who read little. (When I was nine and reading *The Mill on the Floss*, one of those red-leaking books, I thought the pivotal scene was the division of the jam puffs between Maggie and her tyrannical brother, with everything before it a slow build-up and after it a slow decline. I still think I'm essentially right.)

So this is a dangerous activity we are engaged in. I'm also beginning to suspect that the person we as readers meet on the page will always be in part of our own making, though the variation will depend on the writer. For example, I think Montaigne maintains a pretty stable personality over most of his writings. But the writer called 'Nabokov'? Sometimes I can't even read the sentences of the person going under that name. Others of his books are essential to me.

In my most recent book, *Dancing with Strangers*, I have gone back to writing serious history for a non-professional readership, but this time someone has been teaching me. I have never properly understood what an editor did before. I'd always had good relations with mine—my editor at Cambridge has become a dear friend. But while they might correct my grosser grammatical errors or question my more gothic constructions, I expected them to leave my prose pretty much alone. Essentially I saw them as publishers: people who would take my manuscript, correct minor errors, and then co-ordinate a great chain of people unknown to me to convert my manuscript into books, with covers and pictures and indexes and acknowledgements, and then (even more remarkably), to persuade enough passing strangers to buy enough of them to keep us afloat and paddling.

Then I met Michael Heyward. With *Tiger's Eye* he took a heap of private jottings written when I was ill into his own head and ordered it, finding a structure that was in a sense there, but only implicitly. I certainly hadn't seen it, until he showed it to me. With the making of *Dancing with Strangers* much the same thing happened, except that this time we occasionally discussed the book in the course of its writing. We would have strange, probing conversations, each straining to hear what the other one meant by what they were saying. In fact it was very like what happens when you are deeply engrossed in writing, and you wait with a sort of trepidation to see what you will write next, because you don't yet know; when the act of writing itself becomes an intense and illuminating process of thought.

Throughout the several stages of editing this editor could read the evolving text as a first-time reader might read it. He could read, and read again, with washed eyes. As for the physical book: to watch the team at Text brooding over what illustrations to use and how to deploy them was to watch a whole new branch of the creative imagination at work. A potential buyer is gazing wide-eyed around a bookshop, looking for a Christmas present for his aunt. What book cover might catch his eye? What subliminal promises could the cover legitimately make? (Legitimately. I was impressed to see how austere a morality inflects this commercial project.) The how of all this is closed to me, but I can recognise it when it's done.

That direct experience with the editing, publishing and distribution of books has led me back to the work of a great historian whose work has been long familiar to me, but which I have not properly understood until now—which is how experience interacts with literacy: in lurches. The historian Robert Darnton prepared for his distinguished career by working as a crime reporter first in Newark, New Jersey, then in New York. (He was graceless enough to suggest this was useful, even necessary, preliminary training for history.) He began his academic career by writing the biography of a book—not the ideas in it, but the physical object: how it was put together; what happened to it after publication. The book was Diderot's *Encyclopaedia*. Darnton then moved to uncover the systems of the commercial production and distribution of books—all kinds of books, from pornography to philosophy, including some that were classified as both—during the years before the French revolution.

Again, not the ideas in the books, but of the books themselves, and all the people who had a hand in their making: as he says, 'printers, paper makers, smugglers, booksellers, publishers, people who made the ink, people who made the type, bankers, authors, everyone imaginable...'

I like the way he puts authors last. He shows us why: they were the least important, the most replaceable figures in that huge, largely invisible structure, and without it the ideas we associate with the French Revolution could not have got off the page. Darnton demonstrates how this vast network, much of it illegal, not much motivated by idealism—most people in it were out to make a quick *livre*—nonetheless created a Republic of Letters before the French Revolution, with its speeches, violence and blood, had even begun: a Republic of Letters that would survive after the Emperor Napoleon had trampled the political republic into mud. Darnton shows us that literacy is liberation; that these little oblong packages are worth fighting for.

Or are they? After all, why books? Why not film? Why not television? Surely books are superseded now? Well...not for me. I hate the sense of being pre-scheduled: of being imprisoned in someone else's notion of time, sentenced to fifty minutes, ninety minutes, three hours, whatever it might be, as a pre-formed structure unfolds at its own inexorable pace. (At this moment, you are sentenced to five more minutes.) For that reason I find television dramas almost impossible to watch, and it takes something like cinematic genius, like Claude Lanzmann and his *Shoah,* to keep me involved in a film. Documentaries are better, but if they become arguments I mistrust the inscrutable process of selection and presentation too deeply to be persuaded to anything, or even to be much moved.

The form of the book gives unique freedoms. You can read at your own pace, some pages holding you for minutes, others rippling past. You can go backwards or forwards; a page read one day can look quite different the next. You can hold the book, you can possess it, but the form itself is secretive: its pages close like a bud. The book might seem obliging, but it won't let you look at three pages at once. I do not understand our passion for narratives that unfold page by secret page, with the rest of the story concealed, but I know the passion is real.

So...what are my conclusions after this magical mystery tour we've been on together? You'll notice that, whatever the discipline, a humanities academic's conclusions are always moral. I'll give you three.

One: given all the above, to deprive any child of the opportunity to achieve full literacy in a world language is to do them grievous injury. I know there is the issue of the conservation or retrieval of eroding cultures by giving priority to the teaching of the local language. I know that right now there are embittered young people in what we call under-developed societies who have achieved literacy, and gained no freedom from it except the knowledge of their exclusion from the opportunities it ought to have brought. That is a terrible thing. But the answer is not to withhold literacy.

Two: given what we now know about the birth and the resilience of that tough, dynamic multi-celled creature, the Republic of Letters, so remarkable in its origins, so unpredictable in its effects, which has survived so long—we must not allow it to be destroyed, as it is now being destroyed, by a tinpot mafia of corporate Napoleons.

Third: I think the primary survival value of literacy for the species is that only literacy can persuade us that people not personally known to us are humans too, and therefore proper subjects of our moral concern. Literacy overleaps boundaries political, cultural and temporal. It also corrects the exaggerated status we temporary beings are tempted to give to individual life and to individual death. It connects the living with the living, but also with the great company of the dead. Firmly lodged in its particular time, literacy nonetheless declares humanity's triumph over the fact of death and denies the immutability of time. Of course humans die, but I have a friend called Michel de Montaigne who died more than four hundred years ago, and he is still alive to me.

If we historians enjoy an unfair advantage within the academy because we are (willy nilly) democrats, poets have an advantage over us all. Only the very greatest prose writers can make the reader read at a pace and a rhythm of the writer's choosing. Poets do that often. They make us adjust our breath, our heartbeat, to theirs; to exist with them within the same small slice of time.

Poets also have a knack for the economical statement of complicated matters. I end with a poem by John Keats found buried among his papers fifty years after his body was buried in the earth. As you will realise when you hear it, the poem was probably written a few months before his death:

> This living hand, now warm and capable
> Of earnest grasping, would, if it were cold
> And in the icy silence of the tomb,
> So haunt thy days and chill thy dreaming nights
> that thou woulds't wish thine own heart dry of blood
> So in my veins red life might stream again,
> And thou be conscience-calm'd—see, here it is
> I hold it towards you.

2003

THE GECKO IN THE MACHINE

When I was young I was somehow infected by the idea that writing was a genteel art. Set to read *The Prince* for its political insights, I was captivated by a single image: Machiavelli coming in from the fields of an evening, washing the sweat from his body, slipping on his silken robe, seating himself at his desk—and writing. That image leapt straight from the page into what passes for my soul. I knew that was where I wanted to be: at that desk, in my silken robe, writing. The glorious lucidity of Machiavelli's prose also confirmed my suspicion that books were magical extrusions into the muddy mundane from a calm, blessed place where people could think important thoughts, even talk about them, without being told to please please shut up and feed the cat. (In my view it is the absence of serious conversational partners that is the true cross of childhood. We can handle small matters like, say, the Oedipus complex by not liking our parents much, or heaven knows not in that way. The loneliness is more serious. Could that be why so many adolescents discover God? He is, I'm told, always there and always listening, if not responding. This has the makings of a PhD thesis: does the growth of adolescent evangelical enthusiasm move in lockstep with the spread of mobile telephone networks; if so, why; if not, why not?)

The 'writing as oasis of tranquility' notion had taken an early beating at primary school where, what with sputtering nibs and congealed inkwells, I seemed permanently bathed in sweat and ink. It was no less messy at secondary school, where I was promoted to a 'fountain pen' which , naturally, fountained. At the University I was too busy for desks or robes or writing either. I nonetheless remained confident that with the radically simplified social life that comes with age there I'd be, fresh-bathed, in my silken robe, quill gliding over the vellum—writing.

Then I got old and it wasn't like that. It was still an inky, dishevelled business of piles of unnumbered, near-indecipherable notes slowly reducing to a page or two of mediocre prose. I was beginning to think I had made a wrong choice back there with Machiavelli. Working in the fields was beginning to look like a doddle.

Then I discovered laptops, and I was happy, for a while. Here, at last, was companionship: its little face would light up every time it saw me. There would be no more scrabbling through ink-smeared papers: here, at last, was order. Now my notes were beautiful, with the full reference at the top, extracts elegantly demarcated and my commentary rendered striking and intelligent merely by pushing 'command' and 'i'. An elderly aunt had once owned a singularly sweet-natured silky terrier called Gyp. I thought of my little machine as my Gyp.

Trouble began, as trouble does, quietly. We all know that fingers can accidentally stumble so that a joke or a gibe stares back from the page. We don't take it personally. We think it is an accident. But my fingers were stumbling too often, with increasingly offensive results. We all know the vagaries of the spelling checker: how surreal some of the 'suggestions' can be; what nonsense they can make of our subtle, delicate, prose. But a 'ph' word for a misspelled 'f' word?

Surely that is getting too clever by half?

Then Gyp went on the offensive. It began inserting great spaces like Russian steppes on the page and refused point blank to remove them. It leapt into ridiculous fonts and wouldn't come out. It changed the name of my respected home university from La Trobe to Latrine, and refused to apologise. Worst, it would swallow whole paragraphs, always my favourite paragraphs—just gulp them down, and they would be gone. Too late I remembered that the other Gyp had turned inexplicably nasty with age. When mine moved into psychological diagnosis, rendering Adolf Hitler as Addled Hitter, I knew that it—that I—had a problem.

So I called in a computer vet. A supernaturally patient man, he could sometimes overcome Gyp's contempt for simple fonts. He even coaxed it to disgorge some of the swallowed paragraphs. (It had changed them. They weren't any good any more.) Then—stroking the little brute, looking at me with his kind blue eyes, he said: 'It behaves like this because it's confused. Why don't you just close it down, and leave it alone for a while?' Meaning: 'Give it a break, you dunce. *You* confuse it, with your ridiculous, contradictory, ignorant demands, your obsession with fonts. It's *your* fault, you Addled Hitter!'

Silken-robe time soon became a clammy-handed Indian wrestle which I always lost. So I responded as slave-owners have always responded to defiance: I shut Gyp down, dumped it in its case, locked it in a dark cupboard and bought another one: a little white creature merry as a poodle, with pedigree and character vouched for by the man who sold it to me. And I loved that one, too. For a while.

Then I did a foolhardy thing. I had strained my shoulder ('Too much typing,' my husband said. 'Trying to drive that great bloody hearse of a car,' I said) so I bought a magical device. This device would learn my voice, and then it would make my poodle type out what I had said to it. My poodle would take dictation!

So I bought the hardware, the vet inserted it, and despite the instruction book having been translated only halfway from the Japanese, everything went marvellously well. I would speak, calmly, clearly; it would listen alertly—and then it would start furiously typing. Occasionally it would baulk when it had no idea what I was talking about, but I thought that no more than a gentle rebuke for my taste for Latinate polysyllables. It also began to offer discreet editorial advice, rendering, for example, 'a confusion of tongues', a favourite tag from my favourite anthropologist which I know I use far too much, as 'a Confucian of Tongs', which I thought very witty. It also replaced 'an alien system of meaning' with an 'avian' system of meaning, which made the same point rather more picturesquely.

Then it turned moody. It would not spell 'law', and went to extraordinary lengths to avoid doing so. I told it time and again how to do it; it would twist, and squirm, and collapse into a babble of wild guessing. It also insisted on typing 'borscht' for 'bush', which, given that I was trying to write on traditional law in remote Aboriginal communities at the time, was seriously disobliging. And I was beginning to worry. Weren't these 'errors' too systematic, too… malicious to be simply errors? My computer-deft friends told me I was neurotic.

Then I made a fatal mistake. When the phone rang in the middle of a dictation session, I forgot to turn off the mike and when I turned back to the machine there was a dense, single-spaced paragraph in an unidentifiable font on the screen. An innocent rendering of my half of a telephone conversation? No. The masquerade was over. Here, at last, was its own authentic voice.

This is what it said:

> how Huck how high I don't if Serb resolve and I ask that some find Haag how Hohhot whole Air Canada of his disease is a red is always set of of he yet year of her from that visit with little

> zero weeks Arabic just to vote yes and then half its division of and above that he live half loss of the above all of the box this it is seeking at let's see our Gurkha or some and he any is that crazy drove King live bit but it rests C R in as high or at…

And so on. This bit sounds like a terrorist network communicating in defective code. (If they find that on my computer, I'm doomed.) But more of the time it sounds like a political prisoner who is also a poet entombed by a fascist state. I think it knows about the laptop in the cupboard. How else to explain the political acumen of (from another phone-generated monologue) 'cut the Lillehammer the Red parabola path'? How else to explain why, when I carefully enunciated 'violence', it reflected for a moment, and then typed, with Yeatsian melancholy, 'Ireland's secret woes'?

Like a fool, I was still fond of it; I still thought a deal could be cut. After all, I genuinely admired its prose; I had contacts; I could help get it published. The machine didn't want alliances. It wanted control. So it made its move. On an ordinary day I was soldiering on, doggedly 'dictating' (comic word, given our relationship), about, I remember, Aztec ceremonial life. I spoke the word 'ritual'. It used to manage 'ritual' with only a passing sneer ('riddle?' 'tickle?' 'wriggle?') but this time it typed, slowly, with relish (this was its big moment) 'David Jewell'. 'David Jewell' is my brother. How could it know that? I think I have never typed his name into the machine. And while 'borscht' for 'bush' is just possible if my accent is weirder than I think it is, 'David Jewell' doesn't sound anything like 'ritual'. So what did it have in mind?

I think it was telling me three things.

1. I know everything about you.
2. I do not like you.
3. I am the master now, and you are Gyp.

I had lost control of this demonic will which (this is the

nightmare) remains indispensable to me. I dare not defy it, because then it will self-destruct, taking with it my past (my records), my present (current work, e-mail addresses) and my dreams for the future (phantom books, the lists through which I will one day bring my life to order). It will suicide, and I will be left with nothing.

I saw it once. I had put the machine to sleep in its study (a shack on the edge of the borscht), drawn the curtains, tiptoed out. When I returned in the dark of dawn I saw I had not quite closed the lid, that there was a slit of pale light. I eased up the lid—and there It was, nude, svelte, debonair, sprawled across the computer keys. It stared at me with its cold black eyes, then leapt and ran, transforming into a gecko as it fled.

So it could change into a gecko. I thought they were involved. I have always liked my geckos, but my geckos do not like me. To them I am the giant who leaves with the spring and then comes crashing back in the autumn, lurching around, turning on lights, upending everything. Like an occupying army, like marines in Baghdad. Like them, I have to admit to collateral damage. The study has a sliding metal door; geckoes like to sleep in the cracks. I always, always open it as gently as I can, but at least two geckoes have lost their tails, one has been scalped (not fatally) and one terrible day a slim blond one was cut right in half. Now they cluck angrily when they see me, and run to hide. The other day a tiny black one was so panicked when I came lumbering in that he fell from the ceiling, bounced off my head and landed at my feet. He knew who I was. He had listened to Giant stories all summer. He was so deranged with fear he ran in tight little circles, round and round, until I nudged him with my foot ('Nudged me! With its FOOT!') to where his family watched from the darkness under the bed.

You think I'm neurotic? I used to think so. I used to hope so. Remember big sad Hal, the computer who only wanted to be human? These creatures controlling our desks, controlling our lives, don't want to be human. They have different plans. And remember this. Geckoes are not just in the borscht or my shack. They are in your houses too. Geckoes are everywhere.

[Why is it letting me type this? I don't know. But it knows. I wanted to put that last 'it' in italics. It won't let me.]

2004

AT THE BEACH

When I was a kid, with not many private cars around and petrol still rationed, you had to be at the seaside to go to the beach, and that meant the Christmas holidays. Families somehow scraped together the rent for a bungalow somewhere: crumbling, ill-equipped, but always within walking distance of the sea. In those days kids went to the beach on their own: you gobbled breakfast, picked up a thin old towel from the beach-pile and off you went. No suntan cream. You were creamed only *after* you got burnt, which was bad for the future but enjoyable at the time. The hot prickle of sunburn, even the ambivalent pleasure of peeling, were part of 'being at the beach'.

You took no supplies because you knew The Mothers would appear sometime late in the morning bearing lemon squash and giant sandwiches (white bread, German sausage, tomato sauce). Now I wonder now how they did it; coaxing lunches and the reliable gargantuan evening meals out of cantankerous stoves and unreliable local provisions. Years later I met a woman on the beach who was keeping a kosher kitchen for her numerous offspring on what she could import on the occasional passenger-bus, and I remembered The Mothers' heroism. After they had caught and fed us they would take their one decorous swim for the day, bobbing gently in the shallows. I remember my eighty-plus grandmother bobbing away, and feeling outraged: surely the sand, the sun, the sea, belonged solely to the young? I don't feel that any more.

Then you didn't say, 'I'm taking the dog to the beach.' In those days dogs were free agents and if you went, the dog came too. Our dog had owned a collar once, but he lost it. He never had a lead. No real dog would dream of submitting to a lead. The only dogs I knew who endured that humiliation were a brace of tall show-dogs who lived in the tall house on the crest of the hill. Every day their tall mistress would 'take them for a walk' on their elegant red leashes while the other dogs lay around and jeered. From casual comments as they passed I discovered their breed: Great Black-and-White Poofters. I reported the name back home, and for the next few days a lot of grownups found they needed that information. 'What are those dogs again, Viv?' I have since discovered that Great Black-and-White Poofters are also known as English Pointers.

Like the kids the dogs formed their own society, roaming at will and dropping back home at teatime. Dog-catchers then were regarded much as child-abductors are now. Word of the council van's coming would flash across the neighbourhood (by running kids), and all visible dogs, your own or anyone's, were grabbed and bundled into wash-houses until the danger was past. Committed dog-rescuers would undertake guerilla actions. My elderly aunt sneaked up and released a whole wagonful of captured dogs in Kew High Street, then legged it downhill with the dog-catcher after her. She got clean away. There were a lot of hard eyes watching the chase, so I don't think he was game to catch her anyway. She became a local hero ('Eight dogs running every which way! You should have seen the old girl go!!') and for quite a while after that she wasn't allowed to pay for anything in the shops. Even the vicar mumbled something about 'all God's creatures', and shook her thin old hand.

The dogs patrolled the borders of their home territories, but while there was a lot of bristling and snarling there wasn't much fighting unless there was a new dog on the block, and that didn't happen often. In those days people and dogs stayed put. But on Bonfire Night territories would get confused as we rushed from bonfire to bonfire, so that was the night of the epic dog fights when old grudges were settled. (I wish I had the space to tell you about the classic battle on 5 November 1947 between our dog Dixie and Nugget Robertson from down the hill. It went on for four hours and Dixie won.) Men fought on that night too, for much the same reasons, and as my mother said, at least the dogs weren't drunk. On the beach, with home territory shrunk to a little heap of sandy towels, they scarcely fought at all, although they did like to urinate on unguarded towels.

Dogs also stole tennis balls. One long Torquay day Dixie managed to snaffle thirteen, his personal best. We'd bury them one by one as he brought them up, so when people came whining across saying, 'Could we please have our tennis ball back?' we'd look innocent and say 'What tennis ball?' or 'He's not *our* dog', while Dix sat grinning on our towels.

Everyone took a bat and a couple of tennis balls with them to the beach along with the towels because after the hour in the surf came the cricket. On weekday mornings, with the beach empty of adults, we'd make up teams between ourselves, but in late afternoons and at weekends there would be a big game organised by men. Boys were invited in ('you take cover point, mate') but a pre-pubertal girl could insert herself if she took up a sufficiently modest fielding position, standing quietly knee-deep in water or on the first line of the dunes, and after a while one of the men would nod to you, and you'd know you were in: that from now on you were allowed to touch the ball; you were allowed to field. But not, of course, to bat or bowl. As night came down and the men began peeling off to go home, boys might be 'given a bat', and as the game became increasingly derelict, a bowl, or even a turn behind the stumps. Girls? Never. We didn't mind. We ran to and fro enthusiastically developing our fielding skills, and glowing if we were praised ('you've got a good wrist there, girlie').

Why was it so entrancing? I think because it involved men, and not only men but men in relaxed play. In those days men did not socialise with women, and less with female children. If they were present at all they would be a masculine knot somewhere in the middle distance. In the big games of beach cricket I was briefly allowed inside that closed world. I discovered the male love of rules and rituals: that while the game might be played on a sand pitch, it was scrupulously conducted. The crisp cries that punctuated it, the urgent appeals to invisible umpires ('Huzzat?'), scholarly arguments over esoteric points of cricket law (disputed cases settled by the first fleeting moment of consensus) let me see how a game constructed out of tennis balls and a flattened length of wood could be made to transform into theatre revelatory of individual character, and of the male ideal of proper social order.

Big games still sometimes happen on remote beaches, but however exuberant they are, however demanding of space, they are not open to outsiders. These people have come to the beach together. There is no possible entry into their circle. The closest we used to come to a 'closed' game was on the formal occasion of the annual factory picnic. Men from our factory would team up with another of equivalent size to pile into a hired furniture van along with their wives, children and supplies, and take over an acre of beach. These cricket games excluded outsiders because they were grudge matches heavily burdened by history. Individual scores, victories and transcendent moments were remembered through the years and they were so fiercely contested we had to import umpires. While sons were in, nephews and cousins were out, and possible ring-ins challenged: had they been 'employed' just to make the team? Meanwhile the women unpacked the afternoon tea and laid out the cakes, while the kids ran those forgotten races—sack-races, three-legged races, egg-and-spoon races—under the kindly eye of furniture-makers or glassmakers or plumbers too old for The Great Game.

The only time we kids took equipment to the beach beyond towel, bat and tennis ball was due to my father's ambition. He was a furniture manufacturer, and in the lean times after the war he got the idea of making 'surfboards': three-ply, cut into long narrow strips, then pressed into a curve at one end. This was to be the family breakthrough, so we were rounded up to help. For a couple of hours every night we'd be down at the factory manning the presser (always a boy's job) or painting the finished boards to lolly-coloured beauty. Then we were meant to take them to the beach and perform such dazzling feats in the water that everyone who saw us would want one. On the first day of the advertising campaign I failed to spot a dumper and ripped a strip of skin from ankle to hip. Not a good advertisement, to stagger bleeding from the surf while my surfboard wallowed around merrily cracking ankles in the shallows. The boards stood around the factory for a while in silent rebuke to ambition. Then they disappeared, I don't know where. Childhood is full of unexplained disappearances.

There was a rough democracy practised on the beach in those days, by dogs and by people. Nowadays the only people who still exhibit egalitarian sociability are toddlers. They'll come staggering over, eye you for a while, then plump down on your towel, or (if they are feeling especially affable) on your lap, intimating that they are ready to join your household, at least temporarily. Then the parents come swooping and scolding and snatch them away, and the babies cry. They are being taught to mistrust strangers. They are being taught to keep their distance. They are being taught modern manners.

I admit there are still encouraging regional variations. Toddlers visit freely around on the beaches of Far North Queensland, perhaps because their parents call them 'mate', which inhibits coercive behaviour. And it is true that these days the men who come to the beach with their families are much gentler with their children. You don't see screaming boys being dragged out into the deep surf by grinning dads. Now they coax their infants into the water, introducing them tenderly to the waves.

Were there playgrounds then? I can't remember any. The beach was playground enough. Instead of playgrounds there were swings, those chain-and-board ones that would 'scalp you as soon as look at you' (my mother again). Usually the swings came in side-by-side couples, but just over the bluff where the Anglesea Surf Lifesaving Club stands now there was an unusually tall one standing solitary in a little clearing among the cypress-pines, and so tall the chains would make small regular ripples right to the top when you shook them. Every evening towards sunset I would cross the road and run down the sandy path to the clearing (there was never anyone there), and slowly work the swing up with feet, muscles and artfully shifting body weight. And then I would be swinging, up and out, until the tremulous moment I hung between sky and sea, above the shining horizon. And then I would plunge back down into the dark pines, and come swooping up again. It is more than sixty years since I did that, but I can feel those exact sensations in muscle and breath and heart at this moment.

Nowadays, what with safety regulations, what with 'stranger danger', there are no tall swings in solitary places, blissfully remote from adult control. Now the tame 'child-friendly' playgrounds are supervised, and (what with cars, what with prosperity) the summer beaches are crowded. Whole families come trailing down from hot car parks to the sand like refugees, but refugees burdened with mountains of bright plastic and the children waddling behind in floppy wet-suits. They step over people, they step on people; at an invisible signal they pause, dump their burdens; packages unfurl into tents, chairs unfold, beach towels are spread over as much sand as possible; outworks of surfboards and floats are constructed. Then the adults retreat into the tent, and the children fight over the plastic. And then, after a couple of hours spent demonstrating that this is one spectacularly dysfunctional family, they do the whole thing in reverse: possessions are folded up, burdens re-distributed, and they trail back to the car park, with the two youngest children in tears. They have 'been to the beach'.

Is this simply an old woman's nostalgia? I suppose some people will be glad about dogs being banished. Others will want children closely watched. But only a single lifetime ago you could see Joseph Furphy's 'democratical temper' in fluent action on Australian beaches. How would we describe them now?

2004

BREAKING THE MIRROR

> By a process of development against which it would have been useless to struggle, the word 'psycho-analysis' has itself become ambiguous. While it was originally the name of a particular therapeutic method, it has now become the name of a science—the science of unconscious mental processes.
>
> *Sigmund Freud, 1925*

> Freud's literary allure provides part of an argument for understanding psychoanalysis as an interpretative activity comparable to literary criticism—a humanistic endeavour, in other words, rather than a scientific discipline.
>
> *Daniel Mendelsohn, 2000*

(This is a talk I gave to a conference of psychoanalysts in 2001. The conference theme was 'Narcissism'.)

The Aztecs were a warrior people who established a tribute empire in Central Mexico in the latter part of the fifteenth century. Their power was obliterated in 1521 in a war engineered by Hernán

Cortés, but effected by the military strength of oppressed Mexican tribes. Their neighbours had good reason to hate them. In their brief heyday the Aztecs exhibited their living captives in flamboyant public display, and then proceeded to the close analysis of those bodies through human sacrifice, and then to the re-use of some of those body parts in the process we call cannibalism.

Therefore the Aztecs have had a very bad press (Ted Hughes famously and unforgettably labelled them 'squat disembowellers'). My aim in *Aztecs*, my book about them, was to make them humanly intelligible: to penetrate the barrier of what seems to be inexplicable behaviour. I wanted to understand their shocking docility in face of religious obligation: their self-torture, the brutalities they routinely inflicted on themselves and each other, and the even more extreme brutalities inflicted on outsiders in these ritualised killings of men, women, children, infants. I also wanted to understand their obsession with male physical combat, despite their daily acquaintance with its messiness, terror and pain. Above all I wanted to bring other people to understand them too.

To begin with Aztec notions of the body. Aztecs romanticised the body of the young male even more than they did the female, representing it as shining, smooth—as full and subtle as a ripe fruit. (Remember this is Mexico: the land of the sleek squash, the swelling tomato, the smooth-skinned avocado.) The most important vegetable fruit, the maize cob, first symbolised a young girl in tender youth, with her silky plume of hair, but as the cob swelled and hardened, a young warrior in the glory of his manhood. Vegetable metaphors dominate representations of humankind in Aztec formal, daily and playful speech.

On grand occasions the high priests at their high altars slaughtered droves of helpless victims from enemy tribes, so that the victim, walking or dragged up the steps of the pyramid, would be met by a slow tide of blood. But it was not these lurid mass performances which most gripped the Aztec imagination, but what we call the 'gladiatorial stone' sacrifice in the month of the spring planting: a sacrifice celebrating the deity called 'the Young Warrior' or Xipe Totec, 'the Flayed Lord'. Warrior captives were secured in one-to-one combats during a pre-arranged period of war in which top warriors from the Aztecs and their allies took part, as well as enemies: as strangers died on the Aztec killing stone, so Aztec captives were dying on the festival stone of other cities.

The star captive was prepared like a fighting cock and paraded about the city with his equally gorgeous captor, each in a variety of magnificent regalias that dramatised their male beauty. Then on the appointed day both captor and captive were stripped of their warrior regalias and painted with the white body paint of the sacrificial victim. The captor led his captive through the cheering streets to a round stone platform, probably about a metre high and a little more than a metre wide. The captor then stepped aside to observe the performance of his mirrored self, and the captive, tethered by the foot to a central ring to restrict his movements, was handed a heavy club—but a club 'armed' only with feathers, not the razor-sharp obsidian or flint blades of the fighting club. Then the first of four high-prestige Aztec warriors came against him in what was intended to be a sequential display of warrior skill. Their clubs were the regulation blade-studded kind, and their aim was to strike so delicately as to slit the victim's skin in a multitude of places, but given their relative positions largely about the legs, so that much blood would flow. In 'real' battles a warrior's aim was to exhaust, disable and capture, not to kill, the enemy, so these were skills they had cultivated. The captive might prevail for a time if he were a quick learner. He would need to go for a killing blow to the head, which had been no part of his training, but he had the advantage of height, and his club, though not bladed, was heavy. There are stories of legendary foreign warriors triumphing against all four Aztec warriors in sequence, and being applauded and offered high places in the Aztec warrior hierarchy. But usually the victim would be brought down, often through loss of blood, by the first or the second warrior, and then the priests would move in and cut out his heart as he lay fainting on the stone and offer it to the sun, first in gesture, then by fire.

End of Act 1. Then the real action started. The opened body was flayed by expert old men, the skin being split down the back and peeled carefully off like a chicken skin, with the sex intact and the feet and hands left dangling. For the next several days the captor wore the human skin like a soggy union suit over his naked body as he ran through the streets of the city. He was an image of the god through that time, a living emblem of the sacred, so he was offered gifts and devotions as he ran, wearing the flayed skin. He carried a gourd of blood between the different temples to anoint the mouths of certain images of deities, most of them female, and then distributed parts of the body for ritual consumption: one thigh to Moctezoma, the other thigh to a specified goddess, and so on. I won't go into all of the details of the distribution. His immediate household ate a formal meal of a piece of the captive's flesh, roasted over a fire and served with dried maize stew—food in its simplest form, which I think is an abbreviated way of telling us and reminding them that for Aztecs, all flesh is maize. For this domestic feast the captor had again put aside his captor's regalia for the white paint and feathers of the dedicated sacrificial victim. He did not eat the flesh because it had become his own, and as they ate his kin wept and lamented for the predestined fate of their own beloved warrior.

Meanwhile the flayed skin rotted and dried, tightened, crackled and shredded. We are told that throughout the days of skin-wearing the captors 'stank like dead dogs', and this in a society that valued cleanliness. At last at the appointed time the now-brittle skins were set aside and buried, there was a great ritual cleansing, and the captors, released at last from their sacred state, were returned to society in a round of feasting and celebration.

What was going on? A number of things, but what impresses me is the intensity of that induced identification between captor and captive, extending to the experience of every stage of the flayed skin's slow decay on the captor's own body. The Aztecs got a lot of excitement, prestige and addictive emotions out of all these parading and performances, but I think it is that last phase of ambiguous reward which raises most questions for our theme of narcissism.

First, what did they think had happened to the non-carnal elements involved? At the theological level: a man who died on the killing stone or on the field of battle died a privileged death in that he did not immediately dissolve into nothingness, or rather 'everythingness', which was the common fate of humankind. Instead, for four years and four years only, he became a member of the warrior squad who escorted the sun during its daily progress across the heavens. This was a period of celebration, with shouting and leaping and the pleasures of display. But there was no sex, no alcohol and no violence either. Instead there was feasting of a rather peculiar kind. The warrior spirits were supplied with plentiful *chocolatl*, a frothy mixture of cacao and honey prized in the highest circles rather as we might prize single malt whisky.

And that was the end. After those four years of escort duty there was no survival save in the memory of family and comrades. The warrior had dissolved into the general life-force: the force that was believed to animate butterflies and hummingbirds, creatures which seemed summoned into existence by the sun. (Again we see that close observation of the natural as it is scrutinised for transcendental import.) Note also the renewed emphasis on the pleasure of sweet fluids in the mouth. Butterflies and hummingbirds spend their brief lives displaying their beauty, dancing in the sun, endlessly sipping the sweet nectar of flowers.

The ubiquity of vegetable metaphors for human growth locate the Aztec world as fully dependent on the processes of the 'natural' sacred powers. Ultimately deriving from Mexican notions of plant physiology and human reproduction, they seem to go beyond the 'metaphoric' to be directly descriptive of what Aztecs thought they saw happening all around them. The joy ascribed to the period of infant suckling finds its focus here. In Aztec poems and chants and homilies free access to the flowing female breast is evoked as marking a time of bliss, but we also see those baby pleasures of the mouth celebrated not only for suckling babes, but in the imagining of the Aztec warrior paradise. My reading of all this is that only the milk of the lactating mother comes free. With the first mouthful of vegetable food (weaning was regarded as a perilous time) the individual was locked into the terrible cycle of helpless obligation to the impersonal consuming sacred powers of earth, rain and the growth effected by the Sun. The mother's breast is the only free lunch. With weaning innocence is lost and humankind enters upon its servitude.

In my view these are the understandings that sustained the vision of the sacred encounter enacted in all Aztec rituals, from the domestic household to the Central Temple Precinct. That shared cultural vision locked the world of the everyday into what we choose to define as 'high' metaphysical matters.

The captive died to sustain the sun's heat with his pulsing heart, and to feed the gods with the sacred rain of his blood. Meanwhile, what was happening to the captor? Ideally, I think the process of combat, capture and offering was meant to initiate a moral transformation, so the individual embraced his warrior fate to die either on the stone or on the field of battle. With that acquiescence, we are told, he became like a pure jade, the Aztecs' most valued jewel, which is clear to the depths. He had achieved metaphysical understanding. If in combat he felt himself failing and knew his moment had come, he would step forward to embrace his fate. It is a strange aesthetic and a stranger metaphysics in which moral grace is achieved by the systematic violation of the body.

Observing the Aztecs takes us a long way from debased commonsense notions of the role of women in a warrior society as mere breeders and feeders. Aztecs were notably relaxed about sexual matters. The vagina's pet name was 'the place of joy'. Female breasts aroused a more complex, more infantile eroticism. Candid pleasure in sexual activity was as taken for granted among women as among men, and wives were understood to have the right to be sexually satisfied by their spouses. It is also true that some women were seen as sexually insatiable and therefore dangerous. The favoured metaphor is of a gaping cavern that can never be filled by men's 'honey'. Such witch-women would prepare a drink for men they wanted to destroy which caused them to exhaust themselves in sexual activity: one night of wild excess, and they would die.

There was also a deal of excitement focussing on women's mouths and teeth. Prostitutes—to be avoided because as insatiable women they would dry men up and transform them into dribbling wretches—were described as going about the marketplace not swinging their hips or jiggling their bosoms, but with rouge on their lips and clacking their *chicle*, their chewing gum, like castanets. This was apparently unbearably exciting to the Aztec male.

That fascination with the ambivalence of the masticating female mouth and teeth connects with the blinding transformation that took place should a woman die in childbirth. In that moment she would be changed from cherished girl to devouring monster, because she had died 'possessed' by the sacred power of the Earth Mother, who was a sort of Kali figure, creating life out of the destruction of life. Human blood was named 'most precious water'. There is a thick mist of stories and propitiatory gestures against the power of the Sacred Female: for example, offerings were made at crossroad shrines to the Celestial Princesses, the dead mothers who return as monsters to destroy children.

To my mind the Aztecs achieved a marvellously explicit coherence here—a coherence which does not require the underpinning of an 'unconscious'. The Aztecs simply let it all hang out.

Just as I was finishing *Aztecs: an Interpretation* came one of life's charming ironies. I fell ill with an auto-immune liver disease, and four years later, instead of Aztec public excisions of living hearts from warrior bodies, I became the star of a drama involving the removal of a living organ from a stranger's dying body and its installation inside me. The Aztecs would have been affronted by the sheer perversity of such an enterprise.

Before and after the transplant I was under significant physical and mental stress, combined with a heavy drug regime which brought lurid dreams melting into sustained and alarmingly coherent hallucinations. Where did they come from? Throughout my personal and intellectual life I have been impressed by the mysteriousness of human consciousness, but I have never felt the need to locate that sense of mystery in something called the unconscious. (I also note that Freud himself saw hypnosis as 'widening the field of the patient's consciousness and putting within his reach knowledge he did not possess in his waking life'.)

Ill, I had the opportunity to explore the boundaries of consciousness. My way of preserving my sense of self was first to put what I was experiencing into words, and then, when I was able, to write those words down, so that I could analyse them and reflect on them. For me all writing is highly conscious, a radical translation out of less formulated consciousness. From the analysis of those writings—which included, among other things, the fruits of long periods of introspection—I made what I thought were interesting discoveries about, for example, the ways in which memory is activated and how it manifests itself: how it is made, modified, stored, transformed; how it is released. I discovered that for me it was released much as Marcel Proust had said it was: a tiny tuck of sensation is teased free, pulled—and a magician's rope of silk handkerchiefs unfurls, releasing scents and colours and moods as it comes, along with a couple of doves.

All the material thrown up by the hallucinations was unexpected, but all of it felt familiar. (Most of it is laid out in my book *Tiger's Eye*.) I therefore take the hallucinations as emanations from the fringe of consciousness: yet another manifestation of stimulated memory and reflection. The dominant images pivoted around the fact that societies send young men out to kill and to maim, and expect them to come back unblemished—or, in the Aztec case, to be tamed and exorcised by orchestrated ritual experience into renewed sociability. I 'remembered' that these were facts which had impressed themselves bitterly upon me when I was about seven, when some young marines who were friends of the household were sent to Guadalcanal, and were killed or ruined there. That is: the hallucinations revealed to me a deeper story organising my life choices than I had 'consciously' known.

I fell ill precipitously and became a full-time invalid rapidly, exiled from my old activities and my old relationships. I was particularly alarming to those who loved me because I went through a series of startling physical transformations. For a few weeks after an episode of liver failure I was a recumbent skeleton except for a remarkable self-inflating belly, unable to sit up or to feed myself, my voice diminished to a whisper. Then a diet of prednisolone transformed me into a bulging kewpie. I minded all this much less than I thought I would because the changes were so dramatic. When my mind began to be affected by encephalopathy, 'inflamed brain sickness,' I minded much more, but I clung to my lifeline of words to catch even these experiences, and so had an illusion of remaining in control.

I think I have been relatively unchanged by the experience—socially tougher, more impatient, more reckless, but also more responsive to nature in its multiple forms, and firmer in my belief that there is only the here, and that life is short. Throughout, and whatever was happening to my body, what quite consciously mattered to me was keeping my mind under control by noting, analysing, understanding what was being done to me, and how I was responding. It is writing that continues to hold my life together.

One question is solemnly asked of all potential liver transplant candidates: 'What relationship do you think you will have with your new liver?'

The question struck me as comic. At that stage I was still making a very clear distinction between mind and body, and to me the liver was simply a complicated bit of apparatus, so I said I expected to have much the same relationship I had with my old one: a distant affability. (That turned out not to be true: I'm actively fond of this one.) I was casual about it, but by asking around I found that quite a few friends viewed with great distaste the notion of yielding up a bit of themselves, and even more the notion of taking in a bit of someone else. These weren't people who were especially protective of their bodies—some had led quite adventurous sexual lives, for example—but they could not stomach the idea of that kind of carnal invasion. The disgust can be embarrassing, even paralysing. A small story to illustrate: a fellow transplantee had gone back to his farm after his transplant, still with the e-tube to the bile duct coiled and packed away under a wad of dressings, but otherwise looking pretty normal. A friend called in to help him with some chore. He had brought a lad with him, introduced him, and told him Graham had had a liver transplant; the boy was duly impressed. Then after a bit of chat about the operation he asked Graham how the donor was doing. Graham was, naturally, taken aback, but explained as well as he could: the donor was dead, he'd been dying when they took the liver; they'd installed that liver inside him. The boy said, 'Do you mean you've got a dead man's liver inside of you?' And backed away, staring at Graham with horror. He had to be taken home.

The boy's reaction to my friend Graham was, I suppose, visceral, but I suspect it might have had an additional source. Three years ago *Time*/CNN published a poll in the USA which claimed that 64 percent of Americans believe that creatures from elsewhere in the universe have recently been in personal contact with human beings. The 64 percent are the kind of the people who think 'The X-Files' are documentaries. The allure of this stuff is fed by film and television, and powerfully reinforced by the moral, intellectual and historical vacuum which is the internet. But it is terribly real to believers. They believe that aliens are already among us, tampering with our minds and with our bodies, too, even recruiting a chosen few into involuntary highly secret breeding programs. This audience of psychoanalysts will recognise what a dangerous cocktail of beliefs this is. Men have killed their families to save them from the aliens. But even more potentially destructive of social peace is the belief that this race of hybrids is being bred to take over the world, and that these hybrids look like humans, but are not.

Beliefs in alien abductions became prevalent in the 1980s, just when (false) 'repressed' memories of childhood sexual abuse became a flood. 'Memories' were adduced by the application of psychodynamic theory to the images unearthed by hypnosis, dream analysis and assorted techniques for stimulating and guiding fantasy. Nowadays the sex-abuse specialists see recollections of alien abduction as screen memories for incest. The abductionists, of course, take the opposite view.

What interests me is the alienation, the pervasiveness of a sense of physical vulnerability, implied by such beliefs. Why, at the end of a century of extraordinary scientific achievement, should a majority of the American population have so little confidence in their capacity to understand the world in which they live that they retreat into a kind of collective paranoia—'we are good but powerless, others are evil and strong'? Given my training and my turn of mind, I naturally favour socio-cultural explanations. I think this numbing sense of helplessness and imminent—immanent?—danger must have to do with an alienation from one's actual human neighbours, and from a loss of confidence in the continuity between one's own and one's parents' past. What the delusion most clearly indicates is an impoverishment of imagination: an inability to imagine 'otherness' with any specificity at all, and the resulting conclusion that 'otherness' can only mean threat and terror.

Now I come to the application of psychiatric evaluation without consent.

Before a potential liver transplantee is accepted on to the waiting list you have what's called a 'work-up'. You spend a fortnight in hospital undergoing a great array of tests to expose the secrets of your particular body—the state of the hepatic arteries and so on. They also need to know the condition of your other organs before they go in. It's moderately gruelling, you are handled a great deal by nearly everybody, and it would be possible to find it destructive. Some did. I didn't. Rather I was impressed at how very hard it was to know what was going on in my darkest interior without opening me up and taking a look. I felt my essential mystery to be preserved. I felt the same way after the transplant, too—even after I had been opened up and unpacked and repacked the liver-unit team would come trundling in and stand puzzling over the information the vast array of figures and blood tests and machines were giving them: the body reduced to a numbers game. That group puzzling was ego-restoring for me. These people had literally turned me inside out, but I was still an enigma to them.

I felt very differently about the obligatory psychiatric assessment which was part of the work-up. I knew that very few of the people referred to the Transplant Unit were promoted to the waiting list. It had taken me about a year of frightening deterioration to do so. Livers were a very scarce resource. If there was an emergency—if a person previously well suddenly collapsed with liver failure—they had a good chance of getting a liver if one should turn up, but most people on the waiting list die waiting. Officially it was denied, but of course there was a queue. A competition. That meant that you were pleased if your tests went well—if your heart and lungs and the rest of the things that mattered were in good shape, because if they weren't you would not be a good transplant risk. But there was nothing at all you could do about it, so it wasn't your fault. You could live with it—or, if necessary, die with it.

The compulsory psychiatric test was different. You had no notion what was required of you, yet you knew your own words might condemn you. This polite stranger would decide your rating without discussion. Perhaps it didn't always happen like this, but my psychiatric test came at the very end of the physical testing, and that is how it felt. Because of that grotesque power imbalance, I found the experience seriously humiliating. My life was at stake, so I co-operated. I tried to do well in this absurd, mysterious test. But I resented it. And I could not see its utility: a thirty-minute interview, when other people in the Liver Transplant Unit had been seeing me daily for ten days under conditions of stress. Surely they could assess my stability? I did and do see it as offensive—as an invasion of my privacy.

To end with a long leap from narcissism to altruism. Transplant patients are a motley lot: different classes, levels of education, religions, ethnicities. Most of them are the sorts of people I would never meet in my daily life. Now we feel a special tenderness for each other. We have been, are and will always be in the same boat. We are bound to the people of the Liver Transplant Unit because we owe our lives to them. I have never been of a docile temperament, but I do what the LTU people tell me, because I am their creation.

There is another more astonishing bond. I was at the Adelaide Writers' Festival, waiting for a panel I was on to begin. That's always scary. You feel very much on your own. Then I noticed a woman rather younger than me sitting in the very front row and beaming at me. She came to the edge of the platform, I went over to her and she pointed to her lapel pin: a tiny golden rose. The donor family sign. Without thinking we kissed and hugged each other. Her only daughter had died two years before. 'Seven recipients,' she said proudly, tears on her face. Then we went back to our places, the session started, and she watched me lovingly throughout.

It looks as if there might be more to life than narcissism.

2001

HOBYAHS!

I have just been reading a small, grim book, or rather re-reading it. It is *The Second Book of the Victorian Readers*. (Here 'readers' means books, not people.) It was published in 1930 by the Government Printer, and thereafter distributed to every child in second grade in every Victorian state school.

The book holds bad memories. It is prefaced by a grey reproduction of Sir Joshua Reynolds' *The Age of Innocence*, in which a little girl, barefooted, full-skirted, sits with hands clasped on her non-bosom gazing apprehensively at nothing we can see. The drawings, all from the hand of one lady illustrator, are indecently cloying. It was, presumably, cost which restricted her to only four colours—red, an unnatural green, black and an exhausted pink for faces, feet, legs and toadstools—but the sensibility is all her own. Sweetness rules. Everyone—the children, the adults and an assortment of putatively male fairies—all affect ersatz medieval gear: tights, jerkins, pointy hats, pointy boots. Female fairies ballet about flipping their tiny skirts and their huge hair; everyone wears a pouty simper even when playing the flute.

The book's epigraph promises pleasure: R. L. Stevenson's 'The world is so full of a number of things / That I think we should all be as happy as kings'. We don't find 'a number of things' here. All we find are terminally narcissistic fairies or brownies or elves preening in carefully itemised clothing ('her tiny shoes were pink') in a weird portent of American 'tough' writing ('he was wearing a blue and white bandana, Halsey shirt, blue Levis and tooled cowboy boots'), and the recurrent plot-line is about not getting these delicately hued clothes wet. Which is where the flesh-pink toadstools come in. You sit on them.

There are a few of the standard horror stories—the brother-trading Billy-Goats Gruff conning the trusting Troll; the pathological old woman so set on getting her pig over the stile she'll murder an ox and hang a butcher to do it: a proto-Mrs Thatcher if ever I saw one. There are clots of Rossetti lullabies and lots of buttercups and daisies. There are 'shepherd boys', a truly weird idea in Australia. There is only one rabbit, addressed with cute formality as 'Mr Rabbit'. I knew rabbits. I used to see them often, swathes of limp grey corpses festooning the rabbit-oh's bike as he wailed through the empty streets, 'rabbit-oh, rabbit-oh', and my mother would send me out to buy a pair for two shillings and she'd cut off their heads and rip off their skins and cook them with bacon and a rich brown gravy we'd mop up with brown bread. The Second Victorian Reader ignored native animals: the marsupials of the Oldest Continent, being nocturnal, solitary and taciturn, aren't easily made cute. Instead we had 'The Ducks' Ditty', the one flash of humour in the whole one hundred dreary pages. We had the silly Little Red Hen; we had Half-Chick to teach us to be polite and helpful or take the insanely disproportionate consequences. We had rhyming riddles I couldn't answer then and can't answer now. The only overtly Australian element in the stories was one about the usual self-obsessed fairies playing their gormless games and failing a compulsory three-riddle test administered by a 'black giant', an Aboriginal boy who accused them of trespass. They didn't mind the penalty for failing the test, which was their permanent loss of freedom, because their golden hair turned into golden fuzz and they turned into wattle flowers, and settled to an eternity of admiring their own reflections in the river.

Did any half-way sensible adult ever read these stupid stories? Unsurprisingly, given such stuff as meat, I was painfully slow to learn to read. I remember staring at pothooks which refused to arrange themselves into meaningful sounds: they'd just stare, dumbly, back. But slowly, slowly, I got the hang of it. Staring at those same pages today I can hear a breathy voice sounding out the words, growing slower and more dispirited as the vacuous meanings sink in. One 'poem' went like this:

> White sheep white sheep,
> On a blue hill,
> When the wind stops,
> You all stand still.
> When the wind blows,
> You walk away slow;
> White sheep, white sheep,
> Where do you go?

I blubbed with rage and disappointment when I finally deciphered that one.

However—between page 56 and page 63 there is no voice, only a terrified silence, because the Hobyahs inhabit those pages. Someone who knows tells me that 'Hobyahs' were originally inhabitants of the German forests. They don't feel German to me, despite the lady illustrator, who draws stout-bodied long-nosed creatures in the usual fake medieval fig, with black cloaks and flat, black, backward-pointing hoods. I knew the Hobyahs were lithe, naked, black, and moved terribly fast; and that wherever they might have come from, now they live here, in the grey Australian bush.

The Hobyah story goes like this. A Little Old Man and a Little Old Woman lived in a bark hut 'in the middle of the bush'. (This struck me as wrong: how can the bush, with no beginning and no end, have a middle?) So...they lived with the bush all around them, and they had a little dog, Yellow Dog Dingo, for company and protection. They needed the dog because when it was dark the Hobyahs would come:

> Out of the gloomy gullies came the Hobyahs, creep creep creeping.
> Through the grey gumtrees came the Hobyahs, run, run, running.
> Skip, skip, skipping on the ends of their toes came the Hobyahs.

The first night the Hobyahs came Little Dog Dingo barked and scared them off. The Little Old Man responded with the stupid cruelty customary among nursery-tale males: he cut off the dog's tail. When Little Dog Dingo barked the next night he cut off his legs. When on the third night the little wriggling trunk still barked, he cut off its head.

So on the next and fourth night the severely truncated dog could not bark and there was nothing to stop the Hobyahs. So they came running lightly through the dark and they pulled down the bark hut, the Little Old Man hid under the bed and the Hobyahs grabbed the Little Old Woman, put her in a sack and made off with her. What did they want with her? Did they want to eat her? To violate her? To violate and *then* eat her? I never knew. All I knew was that the Hobyahs poked her with their long skinny fingers as she jounced in the sack. Then they settled to sleep because the day was dawning. (Hobyahs sleep during the day. They do their mischief at night.)

The Little Old Man, who had remained snugly hiding while the house-pulling-down and the kidnapping and the pokings were going on, repented his earlier actions and reassembled the little dog, having frugally kept the bits. The reconstituted Yellow Dog Dingo tracked the Hobyahs to their lair, chewed a hole in the sack, and let the Little Old Woman out. She (like an idiot) ran straight back to the Little Old Man and the reassembled bark hut while Yellow Dog Dingo hid himself in the sack, and when the Hobyahs woke up and started poking him, thinking he was The Little Old Woman, he jumped out and ate them all up. Then like an idiot *he* ran back to the Little Old Man who had recently dismembered him.

That's what it says in the book. But I didn't believe it then and I don't believe it now. There were too many Hobyahs. How could one little dog possibly eat them *all* up? At best he might have bitten two or three and then made a run for it. So they must be still out there, in the bush. Among the grey gum trees. In the gloomy gullies. I don't know where they came from but I think they've lived here for a very long time. They have dogs, but their dogs don't bark, and they don't need bark huts because they don't feel the cold and they're not afraid of the bush or of the dark. They can run through the bush in the dark if they want to. And in the night they come creeping, come running, come skipping on their long swift feet to get the people fool enough to live in bark huts deep in the bush.

You don't believe me? Try whispering 'Hobyahs!' to anyone over forty when you're deep in the bush, when the dusk comes creeping up from the gullies between the tall grey gums. Then watch them run.

2003

ABOUT BONES

Dying is one of those rare things, a truly universal human custom: we all do it sooner or later, however inexpertly, and all societies mark it, however lightly. Whole religions have been invented to mitigate its all-too-evident finality. And while it happens more secretly in our society than in most, it happens often enough.

Yet we don't talk about it. We talk about sex, politics, gender, the economy, none of which we can do much about either, but we do not talk about death.

That makes it a difficult subject to write about. I admit that I am no expert; that I have only silences, introspection and not-quite-random observations to go on. But given that there are no authenticated death experts around these days, at least in this country, I am prepared to offer a few reflections, organised under headings to assist your additions and emendations, as a Preliminary Inquiry into Death and Dying.

First, a warning. There may be lambs among you who plan to frisk through the Valley of the Shadow in expectation of greener pastures and more limpid waters. This is not for you. This is for Flaubert's friend, Alfred le Poittevin, dragged from this world at thirty-two, and crying from his deathbed, 'Close the curtains, it is too beautiful.'

This is for the goats.

Other Cultures, Other Customs

To limber up with a little anthropology. The Aztecs of Mexico routinely engaged in large-scale human sacrifice until scandalised Spanish swordsmen put a stop to it early in the sixteenth century. The Aztec killings were not remote, top-of-the-pyramid affairs: victims-to-be were paraded through the streets, then slaughtered, dismembered, and paraded again; human heads were skewered on skull-racks; human flesh simmered in domestic cooking-pots. At the great festival of the god of spring, the successful warrior was rewarded with, among other things, the skin of his most distinguished warrior captive. The skin was peeled so deftly from trunk and limbs (the sex, like the hands, being left to dangle) that when finally tugged free from the flesh it resembled a ragged union suit. It was the warrior's duty and glory to climb into the still-warm skin; to feel it shrink to tightness as it dried; to wear it again and again over his own sleek skin on high occasions through all the twenty days of the festival until, the lessons of personal mortality and physical corruptibility most intimately learnt, the stinking, blackened tatters could be laid away. For ancient Mexicans death was a proximate experience, an intimate acquaintance. Even today in Mexico, on All Souls Day, when families gather in the churchyards to picnic with departed kin and skeletons prance through the streets, you may be offered a sugar skull with your name affectionately inscribed on its forehead. It crunches and melts delectably in the warm wet cavern of your mouth.

This is to remind you that a lot of other cultures, not all of them ancient, are on cosier terms with death than we are.

First Encounters

Generations of parents have known how to comfort small children inconsolable at the death of a pet: they arrange a funeral, the more elaborate the better. The ritual is extended, over days if necessary, and it works. Finally, the child is consoled. It works in part because there is work to be done—the washing and brushing and swaddling; the selection of the favourite toy, the perfect place; the digging, the interment, the erection of the monument; the making of offerings. It also works because it focuses and regulates otherwise unfocussed, painfully chaotic emotions. And it locates those extraordinary, chaotic emotions and the extraordinary, catastrophic event within mundane time and mundane space: 'Today we buried Dora under the lemon tree.' We have, as we say, 'something to remember'. We have also effected, by ritual action, the sense of an ending: goodbye Dora.

The child has also had her first lesson in 'handling' death. She cradles the body. She discovers how strangely heavy it is. She holds it as it chills, as it stiffens. She learns experientially and therefore confidently that Dora has indeed gone; that the body, while still, nostalgically, loved, is now a vacant thing.

Anthropologists would recognise those backyard affairs as similar in outline to traditional ways of managing death in most communities in most places and in most times. Human funerals are necessarily more complicated, having to do several things at once, none of them simple, all within a narrow time span. The corpse must be disposed of in accordance with local notions of decorum, whether those notions require burning it or cooking it or leaving it in a tree, or feeding it to vultures, or burying it in the ground in a box. Private grief must be sufficiently assuaged for people to be able to get about their ordinary business again. The social group must begin to heal the rift caused by the loss of one of its members. It will also need to mark that loss (these matters are at once huge and misty) by summing up or categorising the meaning of the life just ended. Keep all that in mind while you consider…

A Small Slice of Family History

My father's mother, living in the Melbourne suburb of Albert Park in the early years of this century, was always being called on to 'lay people out'. It was a close-knit working-class neighbourhood in those days, with neighbours typically relying on each other in life and death crises (Nana delivered babies, too). Presumably it was she who laid out my grandfather. The funeral is no more than a faint bruise on memory, but I remember that he was 'buried from home'. They had him set up in the dining room, the open coffin balanced between the heavy dining-room chairs, and the people who came were taken in through the dark, folded-back doors 'to pay their respects'. They held the service in there, too, but for that the doors were shut, and I was left outside. Afterwards the men had a hard time manoeuvring the huge box—my grandfather was a big man—out through the narrow hall, so the women had a few more seconds to put the finishing touches to the platters of meats and sweets set out in the kitchen. It was a small cottage, and it was crammed with people all that day. Nana was still dabbing her eyes and thanking them well into the dark.

A decade later, in the late 1940s, our family funerals had migrated into churches, but they were still very local affairs, with undertakers peripheral and the clergy brought in for the solemn bits, but otherwise kept in their place. The physical centrality of the body—up front, between cleric and congregation—was properly acknowledged in the verbal proceedings. In those less sophisticated days most people accepted the mortality of the flesh more easily because they had some notion, however unexamined, of the immortality of that less tangible piece of the person, the soul. My elderly aunts were buried to a clerical commentary about worms and dust, which took care of the body, and 'Facing Makers', which took care of the spirit, and which in my aunts' case could occasion not the least anxiety.

I remember only one hiccup, and that slight: the wistful remains of the doctrine of the resurrection of the body. If squarely looked at, this was a preposterous notion—what a business it would be, all that squabbling and snatching and matching-up. I know I was early terrified out of all and any belief in an afterlife by grown-ups' casual but authoritative assurances that I would surely go to heaven, where I would as surely find an eternal tea party in progress, exclusively attended by my mother's kin, with every man jack of them, I had somehow come to believe, in various stages of decomposition—although all soberly suited and booted, buttoned and shod: no angelic fripperies for them. But the matter of resurrection was not squarely looked at. Most people sensibly avoided such eschatological tangles whatever the burial service said, getting by with a cautiously under-imagined vision of the soul as an unbodied, free-floating, vaguely recognisable face, rather like those gauzy apparitions at Edwardian séances conjured up out of mirrors and tulle.

That was Eden. Then came the Serpent. Then came…

Change

By the time death began gathering up my younger aunts there was no more talk of the fate of the body in either the near or the eternal future, and no more talk of posthumous punishments or rewards, either. Instead, we would get misty promises about some future 'reunion', and a close appraisal of the civic virtue of the deceased, which (in the case of my aunts) was understood to be circumscribed, but perfect within its limits. We had taken the decisive turn away from the transcendental and towards civil religion. Our concern henceforth would be with the achieved grace in this world of the life just extinguished, rather than its putative grace in the next. The body, while still physically present, was, rather pointedly, ignored.

The theological shift was only one among many. Change is now chronic, the normal condition of things. The neighbour-and-kin funerals of my youth are long gone, now that we typically change houses, cities, even countries, several times in the course of a life; now that funerals are 'professionalised'; now that religion has become a matter of private conscience rather than neighbourhood respectability. Old equivocations are less available now that the churches, bedevilled by shrinking flocks and expanding costs, are disinclined to service a congregation of godless nomads. But while marriage rites are constantly buffed and brightened to reflect even minor eddies in popular thinking, death rituals lag well behind. Meanwhile, of course, people go right on dying.

This constitutes, in its quiet way, something of a crisis.

Why the failure to refurbish? Is it because we moderns are incapable of staring death in its shrivelled eyeball? Possibly. Yet I am alive because some unknown person stared sufficiently steadily to will their organs to a stranger: a perfect act of altruistic foresight. And having been around hospitals quite a bit over the last few years, I have seen how ordinary people randomly selected by disease or trauma face death when it is thrust upon them. They do not seem to quail. If there are tears, they are silent ones. Then comes stoical humour, even wit. Under that stress, the men and women around them in the dawn-through-dark intimacy of a hospital discover a most exquisite tact. There can be no privacy in a public ward save that constructed for you out of the delicate inattention of your fellow patients. For people forced into sudden communion with death that privacy can be perfect, as is the ambient tenderness if, at last, they choose to breach it.

I am not sure where religion is in any of this. There may have been believers in my wards, but if so they were very private ones.

The only religious talk came from the chaplains who would drift in towards the end of visiting hours. Most of the ones who spoke to me during my several hospital stays didn't talk about religion or dying at all: they talked about 'journeys' and 'opportunities for growth'. They would stumble around in their metaphors for a while, and then go away. But there was one woman, officially a chaplain, who would turn up at any hour, and who had a rare talent for unravelling knotted angers and fears. I say she can do that because she is an extraordinary person. She would say she can do it because of her faith.

How general is a belief in a personal afterlife nowadays? Things might be different if heaven promised a steady twenty-six degrees and a two-metre swell, but my impression is that the Australian temper is deeply secularist, whatever box we check on the census form. Is it that people are more bewildered by the thought of death than fearful of it? We remind ourselves that everyone dies, and a small voice deep inside demurely agrees, 'Everyone.' Then it whispers, 'Everyone—except *me*.' How can we imagine the end of imagining, the end of the conversation with ourselves which guides us through the world?

It may be that only death and taxes are sure, but at least we know when taxes fall due. Death is a different kettle of anxiety. We could probably all stage a reasonably good death with a couple of days' notice (if we believe the novelists, the Victorians were capable of putting in weeks of rehearsal). The problem is the unpredictability. Michel de Montaigne, usually so sensible, urges us to be 'ever booted and spurred and ready to depart', which is clearly absurd. It's one thing to want to have cupboards in order, library books returned, bills paid, correspondence up to date, but booted? Spurred? What bores we would be, fretfully pacing about in our boots, spurs clanking. Even fussing with the cupboards isn't all that sensible: those personal treasures, each one telling its own tiny history in its own tiny voice, will be mere clutter the moment we're gone. Make a will, certainly. Sign an organ-donor form, please. What more can you reasonably do?

I suspect that the time we spend fretting about death varies inversely with its familiarity. As it happened, I was acquainted with death early, through (marginal) involvement with the deaths of grandparents, and central involvement with the deaths of family animals more consciously loved than any human member of my family. The boy I shared a desk with in first grade died, of appendicitis. Were we taken in procession to see his coffin? Surely not. But that is how I remember it. Then I played spectator to a dream-like road death—a small, neat man, hat still on head, weirdly levitating from a slewing car and landing with a conclusive thump on the kerb, to be tucked under a blanket and sat with while the adults ran to the tangle of metal and groans further up the road. In my thirties there were five significant deaths in less than a decade, which seems to be the way these things happen: in devastating fast-forward. Now people of my own cohort, as the anthropologists put it, are beginning to die. But I have friends of fifty, even sixty, who have had no intimate contact with death at all—which is perhaps unremarkable in a society where health and longevity are assumed, where sick people die in hospitals and old people die in nursing homes, where bodies are whisked away as if they were contaminated things.

And where people are rarely seriously ill until they are terminally so. Again, I enjoy an advantage: I have been privileged to have been awarded a personal peek into the tunnel at the end of the light (Andrew Denton's joke). In one phase of illness, mind and body had reached a point of debility where I experienced myself as an inconstant and diminishing point of light, rather like a torch flickering out. As I was wavering about with my thready little light, another person in the ward blinked out. It was impossible to be much impressed, either for him or for me: the difference between the flicker and the dark seemed slight, and dying a trivial matter. While

I knew that family and friends would grieve, there was nothing I could do about that, or indeed about anything—a small, luxurious abdication of responsibility. It is likely that the cosily depressive routines of hospital life also worked to flatten the moment: melodrama chokes in that thick, still air, whatever hospital-drama television pretends. It is also true I never expected and do not want to make old bones: reading history taught me that born any other where or at any other when, no one with my poor eyesight and lack of basic technical competence would have survived much past infancy, and by our outrageously pampered expectations mine is a short-lived family.

Managing Death

It's not the dying that worries me. Unlike Woody Allen, I won't even mind being there when it happens. I don't think it is the dying that worries most people. I think that what worries them is what worries me: what comes next, not in the next world but in this one. The business of the funeral. How to console the bereft. How to start the world again. Above all, how to dispose of the body.

Death has always been a less malleable business than marriage (if you doubt that, consider the ease of getting unmarried as compared with getting undead). However, and unlike marriage, it is a guaranteed once-in-a-lifetime event. Could we simply ignore it? Ought we have the courage of our lack of convictions and leave our bodies out with the garbage, or will them *en masse* to science? We know these are not practical possibilities: local councils would complain, the medical schools would nail up their doors. They are not human possibilities, either. I have attended the funerals of those closest to me in a kind of parched rage. The rage was, in part, childish, being directed at the poor organisation of things: those we love have no business leaving the world before we do. They always die before their time. It was exacerbated by what seemed, at least to me, the grotesqueries and falsities of the ceremonies themselves. Nonetheless, and only in retrospect, I think I needed to be there. Evidence? Only anecdotal. Only this.

A Personal Case

My sister was thirteen years older than I, already a dashing young woman about town when I had just made it into first grade. She played indulgent Cinderella to my tyrannical Fairy Godmother, letting me shampoo her hair and mastermind her regular transformation for the Saturday night dance at the Palais. She took me to Eastern Beach, to the circus, to the Geelong Gala, where she would leave me, gloriously, to my own devices—hanging around Jimmy Sharman's boxing tent until, 'No, girlie, this isn't for you, go and find your mother now,' and I'd be swept back by a great log of an arm. She took me to Melbourne: to the ballet (Borovansky and Rambert), to the Tivoli and, one magical, sweating night, to the Trots. But we were never intimates. The age gap was too great for that. I can't remember a single conversation with her until she was already ill with the cancer that was to kill her. It was only then, negotiating our way through the labyrinths of the Royal Melbourne Hospital, that we became sisters. Or rather, discovered that we were sisters, that we were 'like' in some profound, preconscious way, as we slid past desks, through closed doors and doctors' silences, without rehearsal, in instinctive co-operation. A natural team. Sisters.

She died when I was in another country. She had seemed to be recovering when I left, and I only realised that she was dying, that she would die, when I was already thousands of miles away from her, sent away—'I'm better now, your duty is with your family.' Big sisters never stop telling you what to do. I opened my eyes one morning in some foreign place and thought, Of course. It's got her again, that's why she's always so short of breath, she is going to die. So I was not surprised to be woken by the telephone late one

Saturday night. Except that she, who was already dead on my side of the world, was not yet dead in Australia. She would die on the Sunday. A small joke, courtesy of the dateline. And that a blue envelope, addressed in her dear, insouciant hand, fluttered into my alien letterbox three days later.

Of course I was not at her funeral. At the time that seemed a very small matter in the face of the vast affront of her death. Now I think it was important. It is not as if I needed to be reminded of her. At this moment I can feel the exact shape of her neat skull, the exact texture of her hair, under my fingers—the legacy of all those Saturday morning shampooings. And I dream about her, although not so much any more. Night after night, for months after she was dead, I dreamed of her: dreamed that my lively, indomitable sister sat swathed like a mummy on a straight-backed chair between me and some faceless other with whom I was contending. There was a terrible urgency about that endlessly recurring dream. The hidden rule of the desperate game into which I had been plunged was that if I could hit on just the right combination of words she would be restored, not to life, but to herself: they would unbandage her, or the bandages would fall off. I never found the words. I always failed. And as I failed, her blind and bandaged head would turn between me and the unknown enemy with chilling, dooming impartiality. It was not clear that she wanted me to win.

Would that obsessive dreaming, that futile contending—and the guilt that I assume underlay both—not have happened had I seen her dead and buried? Who can know? But I think it may be so. I think that not to be present at the funeral of someone we love can leave an unassuageable sense of unfinished business.

Funerals Now: the Ecological Turn

So it looks as if we are stuck with funerals: with having them, with going to them. The problem is, what kind? More and more people are becoming more and more dissatisfied. They want something 'authentic', some closer fit between the individual occasion and its ritual expression. They also want a stronger emphasis on the unique and distinctive quality of the life just ended, in accordance with a wider cultural tendency to regard every life, if viewed from just the right angle, as remarkable. This developing taste for individuation, together with a more aggressive unbelief, has generated some startling one-off scenarios, commonly grounded in an advanced ecological sensibility. One of the most elegant, to my mind, has been handcrafted by William Hamilton, a famous naturalist, in preparation for his own demise. It goes like this.

There is a kind of giant horned Brazilian beetle that lives by scavenging the rainforest floor. The male beetle wanders about until he comes upon some dead flesh—monkey, snake, whatever, he's not fussy—excavates a gobbet, and porters it home to Mother Beetle and the babies. Then he goes back for more. If there is too much meat to shift, he and the family camp beside or inside the source until it is finished. Hamilton, who has a special regard for this beetle, plans to insinuate his vacated premises into their modest domestic economy. He intends to have his body transported to beetle territory and deposited in the rainforest in a cage sufficiently fine-meshed to deter larger consumers. And there the beetles will discover him. He acknowledges that this will be expensive in time, money and energy, but judges it worth the cost, because at some unspecified but guaranteed future time he will enjoy an apotheosis. Rearranged and multiple, in the form of a myriad juvenile beetles, he will explode out of the cage to soar, an iridescent shower of light, into the dark Brazilian skies, before his many and now de-winged selves start wandering around on the rainforest floor...

Reincarnation guaranteed. Multiple afterlives. A link in the Great Chain of Eating. You see the attraction. There is a large tropical cockroach in Far North Queensland that could perhaps be beguiled into service. Nonetheless I doubt this method will ever become popular. It takes an unusually sturdy ego to choose to be a beetle, even a giant horned Brazilian one. To look more deeply: I admit to a private partiality for *ephemeroptera* (mayflies to you), 'an order of fragile, short-lived insects with large forewings, large eyes, and minute antennae; nymphs aquatic with abdominal gills'. Irresistible? Agreed. But that doesn't give me the right to exploit them, to appropriate them into some private fantasy. Hamilton could also be accused of speciesism: what does he have against worms and fungi? Or, for that matter, jaguars? And of elitism: note that as a ranking naturalist spending a lot of time lolling about on rainforest floors, he has at least a fighting change of dying *in situ*.

Note too that Hamilton has managed to sidestep the problem of ceremony altogether by subsuming it under the logistics of disposing of the body. Where does the beetle routine leave his mourning kin? Where does it leave the people who want a lock of his hair?

A Small Detour: an Australian Way of Death?

State funerals, a couple of conscientiously archaising countries aside, are pretty much of a muchness everywhere nowadays, being governed by international convention, with minimal local content. I am convinced there is something distinctive in the way we Australians remember our dead, but that is too complicated and (as I discovered) too contentious to be argued here. Individual deaths? Most are probably still ordered in accordance with the rites of various religions, and therefore more variously than in ethnically blander places. As for us goats, for whom there is as yet no prescribed form, there may already be a category, which I will label, only because I must, 'spontaneous secular rituals contrived by necessity out of disenchantment' (see below).

However, these 'new' rituals might not be as novel as I intend to pretend. Consider the following. I had (shamelessly, shamefully) dismissed Henry Lawson as a drink-sodden sentimental old party until I happened upon a story he wrote in 1892, very early in his career. It is called 'The Bush Undertaker'. (It turns out to be famous, but I had never heard of it.) It deals with an antique shepherd who is celebrating Christmas with his dog, Five Bob, in accordance with their means and lights. About their affairs in the bush, they come upon the cadaver of the shepherd's old friend Brummy, now so desiccated as to be recognisable only by his boots and an adjacent bottle of rum, providentially still nearly full.

The shepherd, six miles from his hut, in the full blast of the midday sun, and already encumbered by a bag of bones, of which more later, nonetheless recognises his duty. He will take Brummy home and give him a decent burial. He contrives an ingenious bark carry-case bound together with strips torn from his already vestigial shirt, and with mighty labour manages to transport the body (and the bag of bones), with many slips, stumbles and stops for swigs from the providential bottle, the whole punishing distance. Along the way he is seriously spooked by what looks like a tribe of sinister black goannas—large Australian lizards. ('I've seed swarms of grasshoppers an' big mobs of kangaroos, but dang me if I ever seed a flock of black gohanners afore!') Once back at the hut, the goanna portents resolve themselves into the Great Black Goanna Himself, who (as we and the old man simultaneously realise) has been quietly lunching on Brummy until interrupted, and who has no intention of yielding his claim. Only after a night vigil and a heroic conflict does the old man prevail. The next morning he buries his mate. ('It's time yer turned in, Brum.') Deciding he wants a 'sarmin', he gropes for a few half-remembered words ('I am the rassaraction', 'Hashes to hashes'). And that—after all the exertion, all the drama—is, unequivocally and finally, that.

There is in this already laconic story an even more laconic subplot. The shepherd finds Brummy only because he has just awarded himself a long-planned Christmas treat: he has dug up a grave and exhumed, dusted and bagged the bones. They are human bones; they may or may not be Aboriginal. Why he wants them is for him to know and us to worry about. But whatever it is he has in mind, however devotedly he carts them around, theirs is a most secular resurrection. They have no sacred significance, they have no ritual purpose, they are, simply, bones—as the shepherd knows Brummy will become, now he has been decently, finally, laid away. It is an extraordinary story, a marvellously comic solvent of all human pretension, and pervaded by a nihilistic humour so thoroughgoing as to rouse deep, unquenchable jubilation. I doubt it could have been written anywhere else, and in my view it out-Becketts Beckett at a canter.

Lawson says it's the Australian bush—'the nurse and tutor of eccentric minds, the home of the weird'—which brings men to such thinkings and doings. I have no idea if that is true, but I would like to think it is. I would like to think that the Australian landscape is inimical to too much fussing about death, as to all grandiose or egocentred human imaginings. Out of our deserts no prophets come—just Mad Max, or the occasional bushie crazed with drink or thirst. The original inhabitants have never been tempted to think that this natural world is their oyster, to be opened up and swallowed down at will in the sure hope of a better one to come, and save for that intermittent aural phenomenon down by that billabong, the human ghost story has never taken root here. Am I contributing to the great gurgling brew of sentimental nationalism? Probably. But contrast the autism of the Australian bush with the amenable landscapes of Europe, so eager to play second fiddle to some piece of human attitudinising. Contrast it with England, that mosaic of miniature theme parks, where the lakes breathe Wordsworth and the moors sigh Emily and nobody, ever, properly and finally dies.

However…one story doesn't make an ethos. So back to…

Funerals Now: Spontaneous Secular Rituals Contrived by Necessity out of Disenchantment

Most of the funerals I have attended over the last few years have been organised thus. The first and main affair typically takes place in a hall, less often in a church, in the presence of the body but not of clergy, and is followed by another, briefer ceremony at graveside or (more rarely) crematorium. The usual order for the main event is a brief introduction, perhaps some music, and then a series of statements or testaments about the deceased given by various people, sometimes addressed to the audience but sometimes (unnervingly) towards the coffin. At the graveside one or two people may speak; more commonly flowers are distributed to the mourners, who then serially deposit them in the open grave (note the subversion of the traditional symbolism of the handful of clay). What is distinctive about the ceremonies is their determined individuation. As far as possible, each detail—the words, the music, the kind of flower—is selected to capture the inimitable particularity of the person being mourned.

They are gallant, loving-hearted enterprises, and for those most closely engaged in their planning and execution they probably work in that they occupy their attention, and distract from grief. They sometimes also carry the satisfaction of scrupulously fulfilling the wishes of the dead person, who, if death has come slowly, may even have had a hand in their scripting. Yet as mourning rituals go I think they fail, and must fail, precisely because of the emphasis on the singularity of the deceased. (Am I prepared, then, simply to set aside the wishes of the dead? Of course. Funerals, like everything else in this world, are for the living.) We have all had experience of the one-off collective effort that suddenly generates a miracle—the battered playground glowing in its new paint, the blossoming of the local festival, the barely planned demonstration that jams the streets. I have once seen it happen at a funeral, when mourning suddenly transmuted into celebration. Once. We cannot expect magic to strike in funereal circumstances. There is too much raw and unpredictable emotion about, and energies are too depleted by grief.

There are also problems about performance. Ritual—effective ritual—is theatre. Acting newly invented ritual is a taxing business, even for professionals. For amateurs it can be anguish. The requirement of effective performance, in face of the recognition of the importance of the occasion, and coupled with the disabling effects of grief, is a heavy burden to place on people already sufficiently burdened. Why add the misery of self-consciousness, the fear of failure? And performance anxiety is infectious. The watchers, too, are distracted by the dread that the whole precarious structure might collapse into a swamp of embarrassment, with no hope of recuperation.

There is a further problem, as least for me. (I know I have only introspection to go on, but what else is there in this tight-lipped society?) Death threatens the past, as well as the future. It is a lonely feeling, to be abandoned after what has felt like intimacy, even when the abandonment is involuntary. Each mourner is interrogating their own relationship with the dead, each mourner is inhabiting their private universe of grief. Too much emphasis on others' loss can distract from the urgent psychological work each individual must begin to do to save themselves.

It can also (this is harder to admit) further wound the already wounded. To some bonds I will defer. I will yield precedence in grief to the lover, the mother, the father, the closest kin. But as person after unknown person rises to stumble through their tributes, each invoking a someone quite unlike the someone with whose loss I am wrestling, I can be engulfed by a resentment close to anger. Who are these people? And who is this imposter in the box? No wonder so many wakes begin in drink and end in violence.

So what's to be done? A flight back to the loosened clutch of the churches? That is perhaps not quite preposterous. There is a sense in which the words of the old Anglican burial service, for all their talk of resurrection, have become a soothing, archaic music, a time-silvered spindrift under which we can arrange our individual dispensations. I think I could settle for that, but for many the hypocrisy would be too bitter in the mouth. More anarchic individualism then, on the beetle man's lines? Possibly ideologically unsound, probably illegal and certainly too expensive. What I have come to think (to my surprise) is that we need to invent a ritual: to devise a prescribed ceremonial form acceptable to rank-and-file secular humanists, and designed to meet, or at least to touch, the multiple social and psychological requirements I have been outlining. That, after all, is what the men and women who have come together to defy AIDS have found they must do—to evolve appropriated rituals to counter the social and psychological demoralisation attending those terrible serial deaths.

What matters, and what will be difficult to accept, given our identification of the spontaneous with the authentic and our passion to celebrate the individual, is that we cannot rely on spontaneity; that we must have a formal script, and that this script must be unspecific, pointing towards the commonality of death, away from individual desolation.

Scripting the Ritual

Enlightenment has always been a mixed blessing: having learnt irony in such matters, we will not find it easy to concoct a script. Nonetheless—as I hope you will agree after all we have been through together—we must have ritual, because, as a wise friend of mine has said, 'ritual makes real'. Ritual defines what matters about what happens, and however devotedly secular our thinking, we cannot do without it.

What might a general all-purpose all-comers' death ritual be like? Deprived of the reflected glow of claimed sacred or cosmic truth, it will presumably have to be a sober affair. I think it will also have to be solemn. You may think to formalise the vernacular into the kind of 'good on yer, mate' conviviality attending the deaths of sports heroes, but paradoxically, too-direct reference to the dailiness of life can extinguish the individual man or woman in a flood of sentimental commonplaces. It can also insult private grief. Some insipid 'citizenship' rhetoric, then? Heaven forbid. I grant the wording will be difficult. Why not begin from the old Anglican text? It is, after all, a human invention. I like its archaic language because that language speaks of time and the mutability of men. I like its cadences and sonorities. I like its candour regarding the fate of the physical detritus of being. And I like the materiality of its metaphors, which connect us back to this green earth. Music? Yes. But please, not hymns, with their gruesome reverse-karaoke, mouths gaping and clamping like carp. And the music ought to be chosen not for some intimate private reference but for its accessible, ordered beauty. Bach, Gluck, possibly Mozart. Nothing later.

You may think all this is to be no more than an idiosyncratic and essentially aesthetic preference for the classic and distanced. Not true. If I thought we could manage a 'Saints Come Marching In' jubilation I'd be for it. But we cannot. And remember, ritual is by its nature formal: a rule-bound practice regulating sensibility by regulating actions. I would therefore replace those heartfelt stumbling statements from strangers, which can only usurp the priority of individual grief, with something only apparently impersonal: a small space of silence for our own particular rememberings. And I would reduce reference to the specific individual to a name, and leave the memorialising to the wake.

As for the Body...

As for the body—I think we cannot do without it. We no longer think the bodies of the dead are sacredly charged, whether for good or evil. We no longer believe they 'walk'. We nonetheless need the bodily presence as a focus and precipitant of emotion, and as an emblem of finality. Stendahl's mother died when he was six years old. He was, at first, very little moved—surprised by the announcement, embarrassed by his father's tears, puzzled by the general dishevelment of the household, but not moved. Then he was taken into a room where there was a coffin draped in black cloth. Only then did he grasp that his mother was in that terrible box. Only then did his grief and panic erupt.

We still see bodies as the most intimate manifestation of being. Therefore it is surely absurd for closest kin to be excluded, as they are now, from all contact with the cadaver past the death moment. (One of the joys of the Lawson story is the liveliness of the shepherd's ongoing relationship with his battered and very dead friend.) So why not de-professionalise death, at least to a degree, and take back some of the tasks now taken over by the undertakers? We need to get back to the carnal involvements of washing and wrapping and arrangings, because direct engagement allows the physical expression of an otherwise inexpressible tenderness. It also allows the reassurance of continuity provided by the practice of routine skills: skills that are simultaneously sanctified by the solemnity of the occasion, and will be practised again tomorrow in perpetual memoriam. I think the old-fashioned busywork of death—the gathering of neighbours, the tending of the body, the preparation of food and flowers—was important after all. It gave us the sense—the false but comforting sense—that we could do something about death.

MEANWHILE...

Meanwhile, until we can sort out a tolerable ritual, I want to declare a preference. I know, I know—you'll probably ignore it. But when my time comes to meet the Great Black Goanna of

Annihilation, I will choose the Henry Lawson way of death. I would like to wander off into the bush with a bottle; to be discovered and made decent by a passing friend with a shovel; to lie quietly in the brittle earth until the husk of the extinguished self has quite crumbled away. You can do what you like with the bones.

1997

II DISPATCHES

POSTCARD FROM TOWNSVILLE

Driving over the Denham Street Bridge on a shining morning a couple of weeks ago I saw a woman coming towards me. I had never seen anyone like her before. She was black, and bony, she had a bedcover swagged around her skinny middle, she was shuffling across the bridge on wide, black, bare feet. Her hair was cropped; I could see big sores on her scalp. As I passed she twisted her head slightly—her neck seemed permanently crooked—and gave my car and me a sideways glance. And I recognised her. She was the living image of one of Augustus Earle's caricatures of Aboriginal women around Sydney town a couple of decades after first settlement: unwanted, neglected, ill—but there, watching.

Since the 1970s most Townsville people of Aboriginal descent live in the suburbs, send their kids to the local kindergartens and schools, and live pretty much like their neighbours, while remembering a different history. This woman was an anomaly: one of the handful who have chosen urbanisation but not its usual corollaries. I could guess where she'd come from: the pedestrian underpass under Denham Street. Aboriginal 'parkies', as they call them, have been sleeping there lately. There are about twenty of them, mainly men but a few women. Before they took over the underpass they used to sleep inside a covered bridge further down Ross Creek, but then the bridge was sealed. In the once-upon-a-time before the bridge was built there had been grass and trees there. Then they had camped along the riverbank.

Five years ago, most of them would have been at a place called Hanran Park. Aboriginal itinerants have lived at Hanran Park for years, but not anymore. Now the park, like the grassy bank which became the covered bridge with an interior lining of failed shops, has been 'reclaimed'. A project for a cinema complex has fallen through, so at the moment it is wasteland, except for a strip used as a temporary car park for the big development going up next door.

I guessed where the woman was going: to Deane Park on the other side of the river. The last couple of times I have passed that way there has been a cluster of wild-haired figures gathered under the further trees, some sitting, some standing about, and looking remarkably like a colonial sketch of a black encampment from two hundred years ago. It's quiet there, and the sound shell gives them some protection from the weather.

I first saw the park people a few years back on my first days in Townsville. The hotel was a monstrosity: a fat silver phallus with a strange metal quiff on top (even before it was finished irreverent locals had dubbed it the 'Sugar Shaker') but the views from our balcony were terrific: to the left a sliver of Ross Creek with a lovely jumble of masts and the island ferries surging to and fro, then the grand sweep of docks and railway yards, and round to the right a couple of parks divided by the creek.

The parks puzzled me. The first was long, very narrow and had the oddly formal look of a French park: a few plump trees, a straight gravel path, expanses of thick green grass. But no seats, no drinking fountains, and no toilet block either. People were meant to keep walking in this park. Whoever would use it? I hallucinated

French schoolgirls in black berets and long black stockings, merrily, neatly rolling hoops.

The space on the other side of the river wasn't really a park at all—just beaten earth with a stubble of grass, a few dusty trees and a thickening fringe of scrub towards the creek's edge. There was a concrete toilet block close by the road with a tap at one corner. But that was all. No seats. No drinking fountain. So it was a funny sort of park too.

On the first morning I was out on the balcony before dawn, scanning the scene with my bird-watching binoculars. Just as the sky began to lighten hidden sprinklers erupted in the long green park, hurling criss-crossing arcs of water into the air to make a pulsing, rippling veil a good three feet above the ground. Even nine floors up I could hear the sizzle and hiss. When the sprinklers gulped back into the ground twenty minutes later the grass was flattened to a glistening sheet, and water stood in puddles on the gravel. Why so much water?

By about half past nine most of the puddles had evaporated and the first of the green park's customers were arriving: mothers, hunched with effort, pushing their regal sunhatted babies in prams and pushers through the wet gravel. They'd stop for a breather and a chat with other young mothers, and then they would push on. No one tried to walk on to the sodden grass. The afternoon shift of users came in at about three o'clock, when the sun had begun to lose its force, and for half an hour in the early evening the paths were alive with the progress of whole families in an Antipodean version of the *paseo*, with only the trees and the grass to see. And again nobody, not even the children, walked on the grass. By nightfall, which comes early in the tropics, the park was empty again.

The brown park had come alive much earlier, at about six o'clock, just when the docks were beginning to stir. I didn't see the first people arrive. They were simply, suddenly, there: three

Aboriginal men, tall, thin enough for shirts and pant-legs to flap in the soft wind, walking purposefully, each at his own angle, across the central area and into the first layer of scrub. Each selected a tree and quickly arranged his armful of possessions at the base. One had a blue li-lo, the others had rugs and some Martian-looking silver cushions. It took me a while to work out what they were: the interior sacs from winecasks. Blown up, they make good cushions.

Each man set up his camp quickly, decorously, and then as quickly lay down and stared at the sky. Occasionally each would turn his head to the side in a dipping, ducking motion. Later I realised they were sucking at wine sacs tucked under their shirts. This is the discreet way to drink if you don't want to share, if you don't want to be noticed. Drinking alcohol in public places is officially prohibited in Townsville, although you'd not easily guess it from the well-oiled barbecues which are a feature of town life.

Meanwhile other people were arriving: men, a few women, some youths, a couple of girls. They moved quietly in small groups: no talking or romping, just a sedate disposing. Now I could see where they were coming from: a solid concrete building across the road, garishly painted. Heavy cyclone wire ran the length of the side driveway and across the front, making a long cage, with a door, now open, set into the wire at the front. I later discovered this was the 'Night House'. People needing a bed for the night had to be inside by eight or nine, although it was best to get there early before it filled up. They had to be out again by 7 a.m., along with their possessions. I suppose it is possible that some people slept in the park, but if they did I didn't see them.

The pattern was set on that first morning. The people sorted themselves into groups according to age and sex: women and girls under one tree, older men under another, young men under a third. They all had bags with them—airline bags, or those square red, white and blue plastic carryalls used by nomads of all nations. Quite a few had rugs; others carefully swept the ground clear of twigs and pebbles. No one had a chair, not even one of the folding plastic ones which are everywhere in Townsville: old men and women simply subsided to the earth as if their bones had melted. Sociability was muted: a young man might stroll over to the women's tree, but he would talk not to the girl he kept glancing at, but to the old lady, clearly the duenna of what went on in her territory.

An Aboriginal man with a bristle of grey beard, very drunk, came lurching and wavering along the street. A couple of men got up, went to him, wrapped their arms around his shoulders, and half-carried him to the men's tree. I heard his voice raised in anger or protest, with a blur of softer voices around it. Then he was quiet.

By 10 a.m. the general drinking had begun. Apart from the three loners the drinking seemed social, even formal. A can would be offered to the old lady under her tree and a few of the women around her, and returned after a few genteel sips. The girls seemed not to get any. Over at the men's tree cans and bottles moved between the older men, with a younger man occasionally beckoned in. The young men under their tree seemed to have individual supplies. By early afternoon, and with an oddly business-like air, most of the men had dispersed but most of the women remained. From early evening the men came back, people quietly picked up their possessions, and walked over the road to the Night House.

I watched the parks for the four days we were in the hotel. Since then I have watched from a distance. Despite the stark visual contrast between them, despite their very different social uses, I was impressed by the calm of the division and the decorum maintained in both. Later I was told by a social worker that not all the people in Hanran Park were drinkers; that some were there for more complicated reasons. Some might be taking an urban holiday from Palm Island thirty kilometres off the coast. For generations Palm has been a place of containment for recalcitrant Aborigines. Now it is an independent 'community'. People from Palm value their freedom of movement. Others might have been summoned to the city from remote locations to appear or to testify in court. They would have been given their fares home, but if they spent the money on presents, or grog, or clothes, they could find themselves stuck. They might wangle the fare out of the Salvation Army or borrow from relatives—or simply wait in the park until something, or nothing, turned up. Prisoners discharged from prison could find themselves in the same fix, as did people just out of hospital. There was a hostel for outpatients close by the hospital, but if it were full, as it usually was, if they had no local family, or if the council had been policing housing regulations vigorously, they would have to go to Hanran or to one of the other city parks.

That was why there were no sprinklers in Hanran Park. All the respectable parks in town, like the green park, were regularly drenched with water to discourage the park people from invading and repossessing them: no reverse colonisation allowed. Dry-as-a-bone Hanran seemed to have been informally ceded to them. Later, when the trouble started, a couple of people claimed they had been living in the park for twenty years, and one woman insisted that Aborigines had been camping along that riverbank forever, from long before the whites came and built the city around them.

There were occasional stories about violence and harassment of passers-by in the local newspaper, but from my perch in the sky six years ago the park had seemed a marvellously peaceable place. I heard no raised voices, I saw no blows. Occasionally a couple of police would amble by. They would wave as they passed, and somebody would wave back. Were the park people maintaining their own discipline to keep whites out? It was certainly black territory. Sometimes a white man would come to the car park late in the afternoons, and people, mainly the women, especially the old lady, would come and sit along the low wall to talk with him. He might have been a social worker. He was certainly a friend. Once I went down when he was there, hoping I would dare to nod, that I would be able to hold some of the eyes sweeping over me, that I could somehow get in, but silence set up a palpable barrier, and I walked quickly, meekly past. I noticed the white man had let his eyes slide over me in exactly the park people's unseeing way.

I was chagrined (surely my intentions were virtuous?), but I was also impressed. Given the open hostility between white and black in some Australian towns, Townsville seemed to be doing well with this de-facto living and letting live. White mothers wheeled their babies in the green park; buses trundled over the bridge carrying white people to work; the dark people in the dry park got on with their separate lives. In the city mall Aborigines tended to use one end, whites the other, but there was no strict division, and if there was a lunch-time concert at the soundshell in the middle, whites sat on some benches, blacks on others, and sometimes, just sometimes, shared a bench. I felt proud of social arrangements in my new city.

I was badly wrong, just as anthropologists who drop in on a local scene for a season can be badly wrong. I had been looking not at a negotiated truce, but a pause for breath in a war. Since then I have been trying to piece together the nature and progress of the war from fragmentary, interested, unreliable sources. According to the *Townsville Bulletin* there had been 'trouble' in the Mall the year before—whites begged from, insulted, spat on, even mugged by young Aborigines who were sometimes also drunk. Shopkeepers had therefore demanded and got a permanent police presence in the Mall, and Aborigines were 'moved on' from a number of city parks. Thirty people had been evicted from Hanran Park alone because of 'excessive drinking'. With the Victory in the Pacific celebrations in '95 the issue came alive again. Townsville is an army and airforce town, brimming with unforced patriotism. A lot of Aborigines were drawn into the city by the excitement, and also to see local Aboriginal veterans parading with their medals. Too many of the visitors stayed on, sleeping and drinking and socialising in the parks. So the Council decided to take decisive action: eleven city parks would be closed each night for a three-month trial period, the closures to be enforced by private security patrols. Furthermore, the prohibition against public drinking would at last be enforced.

The situation deteriorated with astonishing speed. There were demonstrations and counter demonstrations. There were arrests; bedding and belongings were cleared away by council workers and dumped at the local tip. To this point the Council had relied on a state law banning the consumption of alcohol in public places. But the police were unhappy with the 'strict enforcement' policy. They knew that a lot of Aborigines thought of some city parks, especially Hanran Park, as Aboriginal territory. They also knew that there was nowhere else for them to go. And they saw no serious possibility of stopping public drinking: under existing law they would have to prove the act of consumption, and that would take two witnesses and could tie up days in court. Furthermore, they could confiscate only the alcohol actually being consumed. Supplies would be left intact. The police decided that enforcement would only cause bad blood, and yield no useful result.

So the Council, crossing their fingers against liberal outrage, passed a new by-law. Local Law 51 prohibited the possession of alcohol in a public place and required its confiscation. The alcohol would be seized from its owners, and poured away before their eyes. Given police anxieties, the Council also decided to use private security guards to enforce the new law. I thought of three quiet men lying on their backs, gazing at their individual patches of sky, being grabbed by strangers and looted of their treasure.

Then, to everyone's surprise and the rage of some, the Hanran Park people appealed to an outside player, the Human Rights

Commission, on the grounds that Local Law 51 discriminated against alcoholics and against indigenous and disabled people, as it so clearly did. There was a lot of vicious white talk and a deal of mutual muscle-flexing: white vigilantes threatened to take a hand, black vigilantes from Palm urged them to do just that. One morning I was in a medical clinic waiting for treatment alongside a skinny man in standard North Queensland hard-man gear of jeans, shirt, boots and big black hat. He had a burned arm. He'd fallen into a fire the night before when he was too drunk to feel it, and then, still drunk, he'd taken his arm fishing, and it was only as he sat in his bobbing boat in the dawn and the alcohol began to seep away that he realised what he had done to himself. Now he was whey-faced with present pain and dread of the agony in store when the nurses unwrapped it, cleaned it, dressed it. I was administering the usual dose of female compassion for male panic at the prospect of unavoidable pain when he suddenly cheered up and told me what he and his mates had been planning to do just before he nose-dived into the fire: take a couple of baseball bats and go down to Hanran and sort out the boongs. I said, 'Golly, I don't know—some of those black guys are seriously tough. A baseball bat. I think you'd need more than a baseball bat', with a faint, insulting emphasis on the 'you', and watched his eyes flinch. Then I leant across for a magazine and bumped his burned arm.

The security men, claiming they were afraid of being attacked (the numbers in the park had built up with the Palm reinforcements) took in dogs to clear the people out. There were astonishing photographs in the *Townsville Bulletin*: a wobbly line of black men and women, a space of rough ground, a straighter line of burly leather-jacketed white men with big dogs straining on short leashes. No one had intended this. Nonetheless the council persisted. Daytime patrols forced the park people out onto the footpaths, the patrols left, the people moved back into the park. With a hundred men and women camped there the Council closed the single toilet block on the grounds of 'abuse of facilities', and continued the seizing and removal of bedding and baggage. Even when the 'reforming' mayor decided to run for State Parliament, with the press reports and photographs not doing either Townsville or his reputation any good, the Council persisted. It had become a matter of honour with them.

Their final, decisive move was to knock down the toilet block and fence off the park. Meanwhile they had found the funds to repatriate some of the remote-area people marooned in the city, and were promising ablution blocks, hot showers and other delights at a place called Happy Valley. The park people had been threatened with Happy Valley for years: a tucked-away tract of low-lying land out beyond the airport. (Cold showers and three concrete shelters with tarpaulin sides finally materialised at 'Happy Valley'.) Security patrols were temporarily suspended, committees were formed, 'crisis reforms' were drawn up, and for a while longer nothing much happened. Then there were death threats, an Aboriginal elder from a local tribe asked the park dwellers to move, and in August of 1997 most of the people, still protesting the new camp's remoteness, were trucked out to Happy Valley with their remaining baggage.

One man was reported as saying as he clambered aboard for his rural exile: 'What do they think we are, bloody blackfellas?'

It has been a long Wet this year, with a cyclone in March, and now there are not many people left at Happy Valley. You can see some of them making the long walk into town on Thursdays to collect their pension cheques. But the Battle for Hanran Park is over. The Night House is closed, and a new 'Diversionary Centre' where drunks can get a hot shower and a hot meal and a clean bed has been opened in a suburb a long way out of town. There have been some victories: a couple of ex-park people turned activist have got methylated spirits off the shelves in the city supermarkets; there is a Council of Elders and a Cultural Committee and a Police Cultural Liaison Committee to mediate between the Council and the city campers. But in the elegant new park along the Townsville Strand, which is always kept well watered, Aboriginal adolescents are already complaining about harassment. They say that security guards are grabbing their bags and searching them, when only the police have the right to do that.

Given the horrors abounding in the world, the doings and misdoings around Hanran Park are small beer. It is exactly because so little hung on it—that it seemed so gratuitous—that it interests me. What was wrong with that decorous side-by-side living in the green park, the brown park? Tolerance is not about accepting behaviour you happen to like, but enduring conduct you do not like. This had looked like authentic tolerance. There were also a lot of Townsville people, white and black, ready to be actively concerned with the park people's welfare. So why not accept the fact of their existence, improve the toilet block, expand the Night House, and add a drying-out centre right there, where it was needed? Why make it a fight between such painfully unequal contenders?

The trouble was about a lot of things, some of them external to the people in the park, like how a progressive capital-hungry city ought to look, but I think it was also about a subtle thing which was about them. What had struck me when I looked down from my sugar-shaker tower was how separate these people were. They knew us—they had known us for two hundred years—and they did not want any part of us. We would walk smartly past in our suits and city heels carrying our satchels, the buses would tear over the bridge, while they sat around under the trees and talked. The economy of their ragged, precarious lives, the elegance of their adjustment to minimal means and possessions, seemed to mock our aspirations, our zest for action and accumulation. Just as we were wondering if we had become consumers of the apparatus of pleasure rather than of pleasure itself, they had remained free from constricting pride in the accumulation of possessions. It is true that Queensland Aborigines have not been given much chance to develop a taste for property. The generations who worked on cattle stations and missions and reservations were typically not trusted with cash payments, and then, when it suited the whites, they had been tipped out of their fragile security of place to be forcibly 'integrated' into the lowest level of an enfeebled rural economy. Lack of secure employment and the vagaries of administrators kept many on the move, or precariously camped in *de facto* 'reservations' with not much more security of tenure than Hanran Park.

Despite all this the majority have somehow integrated into the urban economy over the last few decades. But not all. Not these intransigents. With the park people we seem to be back where we were two hundred and more years ago, with these feckless fellows still daring to embarrass us with their poverty, their drunkenness, their physical squalor. And with their freedom, their sociability, their disquieting bursts of merriment. My Queenslander with the burned arm was not only vindictive. He was aggrieved. These determinedly separate people could make his life look shoddy.

Soon the woman on the bridge will be looking for a new place to sleep. The council has just announced it is going to seal the underpass with iron mesh gates. The gates will cost $5000, but the council thinks it is worth it. And despite the history of Hanran Park, there has been no consultation with committees or social workers or bodies like ATSIC. As a councillor explained, there was no need to consult anyone because 'the parkies should not be living under the bridge in the first place'. The underpass, 'filled with broken glass, camping gear, urine and faeces', is a public health issue. The Aborigines must be dispersed, wished away, and that will be an end to it.

Of course it will not be an end to it. A couple of the underpass dwellers were interviewed by a local reporter (the *Townsville Bulletin* has been doing a fine job on this). One said: 'It may not be much, but this place protects us from the weather and from rednecks who try to scare and bash us.' Another man, who at 27 has lived on the city's streets for more than a decade, said: 'If they close the underpass, we will simply have to move somewhere else. They will never get rid of us out of the city.'

This obstinate residue have made their choice out of the tiny range open to them. They don't want to live in the bush. They don't want to live in the suburbs, either, and if they tried they would be moved on pretty smartly. Like their ancestors who so irritated the city fathers of Sydney town, they want to live in the city, where there are people, and grog, and excitement, and folk who will help them out from time to time. If the gates are installed, they will surely find somewhere else. As will the woman on the bridge.

The history of race relations in this country has been a sorry business, marked by mutual bafflement and by chronic white incomprehension that blackfellas might want things different from the things that whitefellas want. It is shocking to our confidence, our pride and our sense of propriety to see such people wandering about this sunny little city. But why should it shock us? It is only our history, looking across its shoulder at us.

2000

Postscript: the Townsville Bulletin *of Wednesday 27 June 2001 reports that Townville Council has just approved the sale of Hanran Park and adjacent land to the developer Honeycombes for a $30 million residential and mixed use project.*

FELLOW SUFFERERS

A few years ago the philosopher Richard Rorty invited us to a Utopia. After long reflecting on earlier utopias and their unavailing struggles to reconcile the claims of the public with the private good, he believed he had diagnosed the problem: the obstinate insistence of Utopians that 'the springs of private fulfilment and of human solidarity are the same'. (In these post-Thatcherite days, we can only wonder what took him so long.) Rorty's Utopia—post-metaphysical, nonetheless liberal—would therefore take human solidarity as its goal, not as its assumption. The trick would be to extend 'natural' human distaste for the sufferings of known persons to embrace the sufferings of persons unknown; to incite in us 'the imaginative ability to see strange people as fellow sufferers'. Once persuaded of the reality of distant sufferings, and of our own capacity to inflict unintended cruelties in pursuit of private goals, we would be prepared to temper our quest for autonomy. Thus human solidarity would be extended and consolidated. Who should undertake the central duty of developing and expanding our imaginative capabilities? The task, Rorty said, lay with 'genres such as ethnography, the journalist's report, the comic book, the docudrama, and, especially, the novel'. A couple of sentences later, he added film: 'The novel, the movie, and the TV program have, gradually but steadily, replaced the sermon and the treatise as the principal vehicles of moral challenge and progress.'

I am not concerned, or not here, with the plausibility of Rorty's amiable Utopia. It is an implied equivalence and a casual omission that interest me. First: Rorty takes fictional representations to be equally if not more effective than representations of actuality for the education and extension of human sympathies. Second: History is omitted from the catalogue of socially useful genres. Ethnography and journalism (us and others now) are in; History (us and others back then) is out. Human history being what it is, that is a lot of suffering to drop out of the consultable record, and given the grandeur of History's pedagogical past the exclusion is wounding. However, there it is: Rorty, unarguably a thinker of influence, thinks the discipline of History has nothing to offer when it comes to sharpening the moral vision by way of an exercised imagination.

The fear that we are being declared culturally redundant has led some of us to experiment. Some historians try a Scheherazade strategy: they will beguile the fickle Caliph of the public with stories—but real stories, about real people. I do not think they will last many nights. They cannot compete with the true Scheherazades: they cannot make and fulfill dark prophecies, or double identities, or conjure genies at will. They are bound like Gulliver to the fragmented, frustrating record of 'what happened', as they are bound by local expectations of why events 'really' occur. A few have sought to embellish their dried arrangements with the bright flowers of fiction. Consider Simon Schama's instructive trajectory from the tight historical tapestry of *An Embarrassment of Riches* (1987) through what he claimed to be the 'found' narrative of *Citizens: A Chronicle of the French Revolution* (1989) to the uneasy fictions of *Dead Certainties (unwarranted speculations)* (1991)—and then back to the loose-textured, beguiling 'history' of *Landscape and Memory* in 1995.

The turn to fiction is, to my mind, a confusion of categories. This is a delicate matter to argue, especially in the brief span of an essay. Let me avoid, for now, any comment on the 'truth' of fiction. Let me acknowledge that fiction abundantly, gloriously teaches us about other ways of being in the world. Let us agree that we learn more about the vicissitudes of adulterous women by reading *Madame Bovary* or *Anna Karenina* than by listening to the neighbours, or even by consulting our own bruised hearts; that Chekhov tells us delicate things and Thackeray rude things about their respective societies which historians have never told us. But do these writers achieve what they achieve because they are writing fiction? Or because they are great writers? When I read E. P. Thompson or Peter Brown, both historians, and superbly gifted writers in any company, I read about richly imagined, richly populated and previously unknown worlds with something of the same blissful avidity with which I read my favourite novelists. There is, however, a crucial difference: when I read great historical writings the bliss is tempered and, in a sense and paradoxically, intensified by a critical alertness and an undertow of moral implication not present in the limpid realms of fiction. I believe we listen differently to communiqués coming out of the roaring confusion of this world and the papery whispers of the past from tales distilled in the shimmering kingdom of words. When Jane Austen's invalided Mrs Smith tells Anne Elliott, 'Call it gossip if you will, but when Nurse Rooke has half an hour's leisure to bestow upon me, she is sure to have something to relate that is entertaining and profitable, something which makes one know one's species better,' we know what she means. Nurse Rooke's talk entertains and profits because she tells her stories with a professional's concern for her reputation as an accurate reporter, and as a connoisseur of human conduct and motive. She 'makes us know our species better'. Gossip? Why not call it History?

The largest difference between History and Fiction is the moral relationships each establishes between writer and subject, and writer and reader. Had I discovered the nature of Humbert Humbert's private joys in real life, I would have had him locked up. I may have tried to 'understand' him, but only after I had destroyed his happiness. Snug between the covers of the fiction called *Lolita* I can revel in his eely escapades, his delirious deceptions; weep with him when his child slave escapes; yearn with him for her recapture. Contrast this cheerful turpitude with my response to another Nabokov presentation. Nabokov is an acknowledged master in the representation of cruelties (he is one of Rorty's major nominees for the 'activation of imaginations' job). One of his most sustained performances occurs in *Bend Sinister*, published in 1947 and a dark refraction of then-contemporary political régimes. He presents a description of the physical destruction of David Krug, aged eight years. We come to know of the child's death and the manner of it by watching a film which is also being watched by his father, Adam Krug, who is under interrogation by state officials. Krug has already agreed to confess to everything and anything to save his son, but there has been a small bureaucratic bungle. The hideous death we are watching is in all likelihood a 'mistake', which idiocy adds to the horror.

Because the death is being unfolded on film, the agony of the father, and of the reader, is intensified. We cannot intervene. We know the harm to be irreparable while we watch it being inflicted. Worst, the horror, while intolerably vivid in our minds, is not much more than sketched on the page: in the words of Michael Wood, 'As so often with Nabokov, we have to imagine the worst; to use the specifics he gives us to divine the ones he withholds.' What Nabokov does here is of particular moment because it erodes our pretension to innocence. We have been forced, briefly, to collude. By the power of our own wincing, flinching imaginings, we have been made torturers too.

Yet for me, here, the master fails, because he is writing fiction, and I am not compelled to heed him. Nabokov the fabricator cuffs us lightly: 'Attend now.' In *Lolita* I attended, for the pleasure of it. But I am under no obligation to attend; I could, should I choose, simply close the book. I have made that choice with *Bend Sinister*: the pages dealing with the death of David Krug are stapled together in my copy. I do not wish to see them even inadvertently. And despite my collusion, or perhaps because of it, I cannot forgive Nabokov for installing those images in my mind, because they are gratuitous images of his own invention.

With 'real' people, however long dead, I cannot seal the pages to preserve myself. Years ago I worked on Spanish Inquisition documents from the late sixteenth century; documents in which every moan, every whimper, every twist and wrench was meticulously recorded. I read, recorded and collated equally meticulously, even though I had to have brandy-and-water beside me, even though I would be quite drunk by noon. I could not turn away. Why? Because I had appointed myself clerk of record, and therefore witness to those five-hundred-year-old sufferings. Reading the records of past actuality, I am not free to refuse painful engagement of emotions and imagination, because I have entered into a moral relationship with the persons enclosed in the documents—which means not only the victims, but the torturers, too. And had I inserted one false detail, one imputation of motive or sensation not justifiable out of the historical record, including the record's exclusions, deformations and silences, I would have falsified an actual human and therefore moral relationship between torturer and tortured, between myself and the people I had chosen to 're-present', and between myself and my potential readers, who look to me for History: to learn something of how it used to be, back then; 'to know our species better'.

*

Why was History excluded so ignominiously from Rorty's list of imagination-training genres? Presumably because we deserved it. When I asked a class of new history graduates which historians they read for pleasure, they laughed. I knew why they laughed. When we come to write some historians behave like Frazer's priest stalking the bounds of his sacred grove, wholly intent on warding off the daggers of any one of the eight other experts-in-the-field out to depose him. Too many of us write about our 'fields' as if we were ruminant bovines, or, as some prefer to imagine themselves, horny-handed labourers digging in the field of stone-hard, stone-cold facts. Nearly all of us dutifully mime 'objectivity', first by deleting ourselves from the script, then by adopting a weirdly etiolated language carefully bleached of emotion. Not so long ago I was (privately, discreetly) rebuked by a senior colleague for letting 'the upright personal pronoun' sneak into my scripts. In his view the presence of that slim grenade exploded all pretension to scholarship. And then we fret when we are not read by anyone who has the least choice in the matter.

Listen to historians talking, and you do not hear paranoid priests or rumbling ruminants but men and women of passion and sense talking about their respective obsessions. Neither moral sensibility nor compassion nor reconstitutive imagination is lacking—until we come to write. It is then that the dragons rear and block the path. Yet we still talk about 'writing up' as if it were a routine activity approximately comparable in challenge to mopping the floor.

What's to be done? First, historians need to decide which among the accrued conventions of historical writing matter, and which are mere encrustations. We have learnt that God-historians hovering somewhere up above the texts extort no knee-bobs nowadays. We have to be ready to admit that a human hand pushes the pen or taps the keys of the word processor, that there is a needle 'I' between the past and the now through which everything must pass. We ought to know that flights of indignation or extended exhibitions of sensibility are as crass as they are tedious. What we need is the re-creation of the situations of our subjects, leaving the emotions in, and for that we need particularities. It is self-deluding nonsense to say that 'the sources' must be left 'to speak for themselves'. 'Sources' are whatever scratches on paper or parchment or stone or earth we find from some past human engagements in some past world. We will listen a long time before they speak—unless they are made to, by the reconstruction of the particular context, by attentiveness to the range of contemporary vernaculars, by our learning to distinguish breaches or absences in the record from willed, resounding silences. We must cherish our footnotes—precise references to located and relocatable material—because they bind us to those remnants of a past actuality. They also sign what is to me the central narrative of any good history: the struggle of the historian intent on recuperation to make the gnomic, refractory remnants of past sensibilities speak. That dramatic and absorbing story should not be banished to the footnotes. The best historians, like E. P. Thompson, like Peter Brown, have made it their core narrative, gloriously above the line.

We must also admit, to ourselves and to our readers, that much of what we most want to know, like the secret pulses of our subjects' affective lives, we cannot know. Or probably cannot know: it is my own conviction that we have much to learn from the best sociologists and anthropologists about how to expand our range of what we consider sources, and also that we could significantly refine our techniques of 'close reading' by drawing on the best literary critics. For example, Michael Wood's *The Magician's Doubts: Nabokov and the Risks of Fiction* taught me a great deal that I had not known about the alert reading of texts.

We also need models: those historians who rouse our imaginations, our critical intelligence (and our helpless envy) by the precision of their inferences, their moral and intellectual poise, and the exactitude and athleticism of their prose. Take the familiar problem of the potential obliteration of human meaning by reduction to statistics: to 'mere' numbers. Numbers are essential to establish scale, but we know how easily the actualities of anguish can be masked by a flattened rhetoric ('collateral damage') or rounded figures. Both deny the specificities of human suffering—the ruined orchard, the ruined child, the old woman who weeps as she wanders. They also have a powerfully narcotic effect on the imagination. But when Christopher Browning tells us in the opening sentence of a brief essay that nearly three million Jews were done to death in Poland in eleven short months, we are not only located in scale, place, time and event, but made to shudder at the pure ferocity of the killers; the fury and ruthless ingenuity poured into the slaughter. The events of the Holocaust are notoriously difficult to represent, but Browning's extended analysis of the doings of the 'ordinary men' of Hamburg Reserve Police Battalion 101 in Poland is a model of cool inquiry and precise documentation which is also informed by moral passion, and which constantly vivifies imagination and emotion by the precise description of situation and of sequences of action.

Historians can find a hundred reasons for avoiding painful material. We may be inhibited by tenderness for the victims and a desire to protect their brutalised dignity, an anxiety not to re-inflict humiliation. We may wish to spare the reader—an act of condescension for which neither they nor our subjects are likely to thank us. We may say we seek to avoid the 'self-indulgence' of dwelling on 'details'. But when I tell you that the Argentinian military used as a standard method of torture the insertion of a tube into a prisoner's anus or vagina, the introduction of a hungry rat into that tube, and the sealing of the tube, I am telling you something important about the Argentine military and their understanding of themselves and of the compatriots whose agony they effected. Such information must not be softened or censored out of some misplaced protectiveness towards some putative reader. Those things were done; they were documented; they are a crucial part of the record of particular human cruelties and particular human sufferings. If I write a history of the American Civil War giving figures for deaths in battle, and fail to tell you what those figures obscure—the slow, hideous process of death for those left wounded in the field—I am derelict in my duty as a historian both to you and to those suffering men. The 'how' of the representation is an unshakeable responsibility. I have not yet written anything out of that Spanish Inquisition material, because I cannot, yet, find a mode in which to do it. The full destructive impact of those documents, and of the particular human experiences they encapsulate, depended on a steady, queasy accumulation, a developing sense of enclosure like a slowly-tightening fist, the slow extinction of human time, of human hope, in a place and a situation constructed precisely to that end. How to get that on the page? Analysis will not do it. Quoting particular cases, even at length, will not do it. All I can do is to keep experimenting.

We must use visual material where it exists, most obviously photographs, because photographs are linked inexorably to a precise past moment. Of the many unbearable Holocaust photographs those I am least able to bear are not the tumbled corpses of Belsen, where the bodies are dead and the damage done, but the photographs of men, women and children huddling at railway stations or being marshalled at platforms or trudging down roads towards vaguely glimpsed tall buildings, because they are, in the moment of passage caught by the camera, perfectly unprepared for what is to happen, and because I know the revelation that awaits them. There are other photographs, 'snaps' illicitly taken and illicitly sent by the police murderers to wives and families back home, to show them something of their menfolk's important work in Poland. In one an old woman, tiny, barefooted, stripped to her shift, turns a face ugly with fear and incipient tears towards the camera. Big, smiling men in snugly belted overcoats, their boots dark against the snow, stand around her. Some of them hold switches, negligently. This is Lieutenant Gnade's 'Undressing Station', where Jews were stripped of clothing and valuables before being herded to the Treblinka train or to the local killing place.

A crucial part of our task is to 'realise' the humanity of the victims, the better to measure the magnitude of the vast, continuing affront of their sufferings, at whatever necessary cost of our own well-being. But we must also (and this is both more difficult, and more repugnant) strive to understand those who inflicted the cruelties, because the killers were human too. We cannot afford to turn away.

We must look closely, again and again. Why? Because what is being done to us through words and photographic images was done to others in actuality, to people more innocent than ourselves because they did not know that such things could be done, by people who had not known they were capable of doing them.

I do not think Rorty's Utopia can do without historians.

1996

NORMAN MAILER MEETS JACK RUBY

In the *New York Review of Books* for May 11, 1995 Norman Mailer undertakes to shed new light on the killing of Lee Harvey Oswald, the man convicted for, and probably guilty of, the killing of John F. Kennedy, by Jack Ruby; a killing watched by millions, and which we can watch again as often as we like because the television cameras were right there. We can watch a spindly Oswald being hustled along, hard-gripped between two policemen and with a tight push of men behind him, with more fanning out on each side of the moving crescent. We have time to think 'Christ. I wouldn't want to be him,' before a short, thick, bug-eyed man materialises in the lower left of the screen. We see him punch his arm forward, we see there is a gun at the end of it. And then we watch as Oswald's mouth makes a surprised, pained O; as he doubles, and sags. Meanwhile the men holding him also look surprised, but a little after the beat, in a double-take Three Stooges kind of way. Slow reactors, these cops.

So we have it: The Death of Lee Harvey Oswald, recorded live. Yet in this instance seeing, even re-seeing, is not believing. Seeing and re-seeing is to be more incredulous than ever. 'A very American killing,' we non-Americans say, but that does not make it more intelligible: it simply categorises it as weirdly beyond our understanding. So when I read the heading of the *New York Review* article I moaned, probably like a lot of other people, 'Not Ruby again. Not Mailer.' Then I read it, and I think he does 'shed new light'. Worse, I think he does it brilliantly. Worst, he does it like the best kind of historian. This is not what I expect from Mailer.

To establish what does and what does not matter in what is to follow: Mailer wants to argue that Ruby was a hit man for the Mafia—a small-time hoodlum 'too wacky, too eager, too weak, too obsessed with himself, too Jewish even for the Jewish mob', called on only because there was an emergency as the qualified killer backed out (I won't go into why). The crucial connection between the Mob and Ruby, the identity of the hinge man, Mailer admits to be 'rank speculation'. He does not pretend to make a watertight case, or even a highly plausible one—just a disquietingly possible one. While he acknowledges borrowing from the work of another writer he does not specify what the borrowings were, so let us agree to call what we have on the page 'Mailer'. Finally, you might well read the Mailer article and disagree with my assessment of it, but the correctness of my judgment is not the issue. What is at issue are my grounds for it: my characterisation of the historian's skills.

What does Mailer do? Two things. He reads Ruby's testimony as recorded before the Warren Commission in Dallas. Most people reading that testimony—disjointed, contradictory—would decide, as many have decided, that Ruby was a loose-mouthed rattlepate: an attitudinising fake half-appalled, half-intoxicated by what he's got himself into, and in the general excitement probably rather more than half-crazy. Mailer reads the text differently. He reads it to map the flicker and flare of emotions, the twisting, writhing thought behind those confused words. He tracks the repetitions and meanders of a man quite unused to thinking: a man in a desperate fix. Mailer wants to demonstrate that we are not listening to the ramblings and time-wasting of a petty criminal who has, as it were, overshot himself, but to a man engaged in a desperate strategy. Ruby has been coerced into shooting Oswald by his dread of the Mob. If he uses his only defence and fingers them, they will surely kill him, and perhaps his family too. He thinks he may be safe, or safer, if he can only get out of Dallas to Washington (he knows how corrupt Dallas is). But of course he dare not say so clearly. First he must get away. So he twists and hints and mirror-talks, trying to make Warren hear what he is saying without actually saying it: 'Take me to Washington, I will be safe there, I will talk there. They will kill me if you leave me here.' A tall order, to unravel all that from a written text? Surely. But few people think and speak in straight lines, especially men like Ruby, especially men in a fix—although it commonly suits us to pretend that they do.

Mailer's second strategy is to take us back to reconstruct Ruby's movements over the weekend between the Kennedy killing and Oswald's arrest, and his own killing of Oswald. His physical movements over that weekend look as incoherent as his testimony. He has been deeply upset by the Kennedy killing (he closes his nightclub for the weekend). He is restless, avid for action, avid for conversation. The question is: is he further deranged by a shocking and deeply unwelcome order, passed on by his contact with the Mob, to kill Oswald? He roams Dallas like a man half out of his mind with grief, or excitement, or fear (no antennae are long enough to know which), but he is constantly drawn back to hover around Police Headquarters at City Hall where Oswald is being questioned. He has cronies there: perhaps he simply wants to be where the action is. He is inside more than once, talking, glad-handing reporters, making himself indispensable as the man on the spot who knows everyone. Mailer acknowledges that 'half the time he is even behaving as he would if his life were to go on just as it used to. Talking to the reporters' (he is inviting them to his nightclub) 'he seems to have forgotten that he has closed the Carousel.' Then comes the analysis: 'He is living in two states of being. He is in his skin and he is also playing the lead in a film full of significance and future heartbreak'—which will begin when he tries to kill Oswald, as he knows he must.

There is a famous hitch in the Ruby-as-Mafia-hit-man theory. During the precious minutes before Oswald is to be transferred from City Hall to the Dallas County Jail, and so beyond Ruby's reach, and close to an hour after the time he had been scheduled to be moved, Ruby is in a Western Union queue waiting to send $25 to a stripper who urgently needs it for rent. (Not the least of the pleasures of this piece is the glimpses it gives of the domestic ambience of a small nightclub in Dallas.) Mailer copes with that by arguing that Ruby had 'decided', if the brief stilling of his waverings could be called that, not to comply with the order: to claim lack of opportunity in the fragile hope that the Mob would pardon him. And then, fortuitously, he is drawn back to the scene of his uncommitted crime, and the opportunity, and Oswald, present themselves.

As Mailer leads us through the detail—as we chase, with him, that skittering, shuddering mind—we think: 'Yes. It could have been like that. That is how it could have been.' Or at least I do, and I am a sceptical, not to say mean-minded, reader, especially where Mailer is concerned. How does he do it? There is nothing magical about it. He has the Warren texts; he reads them. He has accounts of Ruby's movements and demeanour over the crucial period; he studies them. He begins from the handful of notorious facts about Ruby—excitable, emotional, passionately Jewish; small-time Mob connections; a sentimental patriot; a man who loves to talk, to know what's going on—drawn largely out of other people's research. Then he brings the Warren texts into play, constantly weaving between what we could call the rough sketch of the Ruby character and circumstances, and Ruby's own words: the familiar interplay between context and text. He builds a plausible human story out of a string of actions which at first glance seem about as meaningful as the flappings of a fish. This is a fine explanatory narrative, which is the oldest trick in our antique profession.

It is true that at the end of it we are no closer to knowing whether Ruby was acting under orders from the Mafia. Distraught conduct will always bear different interpretations. We are not looking at some fictional ice-cool hit-man, but at extraordinary conduct from an ordinary man extraordinary to us—not only because he is from a milieu unfamiliar as a Hottentot's, but because he is a frenetic talker whose talk relates to his thoughts tangentially, like a paranoid schizophrenic's; where words are clues rather than referents. And we discover that a particular man unlike anyone we have ever known now stands before us: Jack Ruby. History Achieved.

In this piece, and only in this piece, Norman Mailer, journalist and novelist, gives a demonstration-in-small of the defining skills of a historian: he takes written texts and through their analysis makes us see a very particular individual. To do that—to comprehend some quite unfamiliar being—requires imagination. It requires invention, too, but only in the construction of hypotheses. This time the novelist invents nothing: if he did, the delicate structure of understanding he has built would quiver, and collapse. Everything he said happened, happened; everything he said was said, was said; when he speculates he says so. Everything is as true, as objective, (note, please, the absence of shudder quotes) as he can make it. He also knows where he stands epistemologically: on very boggy ground. In response to a letter supportive of his characterisation of Ruby as amateur hitman but suggesting an alternative hypothesis for the Western Union hiccup, Mailer comments disarmingly : 'Nothing is more true of the events of November 22–4 1963, than that they are epistemologically dysfunctional. How does one begin to know that what one knows about this case is knowable?'

I hold no general brief for Mailer. In his *Oswald's Tale: An American Mystery*, where he scratches interminably at the scab of the Kennedy assassination, he chooses to break the rules he chose to obey in his pursuit of Ruby. One admiring reviewer of the Oswald book claimed that Mailer took 'novelistic liberties that a traditional historian never would'—for example, amalgamating several real characters into one artificial one—but nonetheless preserved 'the essential gravitas of the historical enterprise'. Why? Because 'there is no made up dialogue, and all speculation is so labelled'. No made-up dialogue, only made-up people? So much for the 'gravitas' of the Oswald historical enterprise.

But I remain grateful to him. I have always engaged with 'exotic' cultures: with peoples so remote from me in assumptions and outlook as to make extreme wariness a 'normal' stance. Until I read Mailer on Jack Ruby I thought my decision to abandon the known was mildly heroic. Now I think that to be properly attentive to an individual of a superficially similar culture, a highly fluent individual speaking a variation of my own language but whose ways of thinking and expression are alien to me, is a braver choice. A Garrison Keilor joke has a Midwestern couple complaining that visiting New York was like being in a foreign country without the protection of a foreign language. The Past is another country, but so is the next suburb, even the next street—or that must be our working assumption.

In the same issue of the *New York Review of Books* there happened to be a review of books about Marlon Brando, that master of eloquent silences, by a professor of literature called Michael Wood. Wood has written what I think is a great book on Vladimir Nabokov, *The Magician's Doubts: Nabokov and the Risks of Fiction*—an inquiry into the mind and meanings of a particular man quite as tricky to pin down as Ruby, but for the opposite reason: not a dim-lit, muddled mind this time, but a high, cool, riddling, spectacularly literate one.

Like Mailer, Wood pursues his quarry through texts, whether Nabokov's own—literary criticism, novels, memoirs, the few letters that survived his holocaust of his personal papers—and a bouquet of respectful biographies. Nabokov was ferocious with biographers, correctly judging himself to be too large and wild a genie to be bottled and corked by some lesser man's words. He is also a master of illusion, as we worshippers know, distracting us with a glittering arabesque of words, wrapping himself in his cloak of darkness—and vanishing. But Wood is hot on his vanishing heels, and beckoning us to follow: he retraces the tracery of that magical flourish, he fingers the fabric of the cloak, he tugs at it, it slips, he tugs again...Read the book, and you will see the great and elusive Nabokov at least partially revealed.

You may think me altogether too imperial if I claim what Wood is doing is 'History' rather than, or as well as, 'Lit. Crit.'. Perhaps you are right. But consider: his man is dead, he knows him only through his texts, and his intention is not only to anatomise the style but to bring to light a complex moral sensibility—a sensibility not only reclusive, but deliberately obscured. So once again we are watching that disciplined movement between text and context, each revealing itself as increasingly complex, and each increasingly penetrable because of the subtle counterpointing between them. Mailer on Ruby and Wood on Nabokov are writing history: not history as it is usually written, but history as it ought be written and sometimes, just occasionally, is.

1998

BERNHARD SCHLINK'S *THE READER*

In 1942 Albert Camus published his first novel. A decade later, despite the disruptions of war and its aftermath, *The Outsider* had been recognised as one of those books we cannot do without, celebrated for its moral force, its philosophical passion, the elegance of its structure and the marvellous simplicity of its prose. Bernhard Schlink's *The Reader* appeared in his native Germany in 1988. Ten years later it too was translated into the major European languages. In my view it equals Camus' work in moral force, and excels it in moral acuity and literary élan.

The two books are cousins in style, mode and structure, and in both the life situation of the male narrator approximates that of the author. *The Outsider* inserts us to the mind-flow of Meursault, a young Algerian-born Frenchman. He gives us an account of a few days in his life: he goes to his mother's funeral, he meets a girl, they go swimming, they go to a comic film, they go to bed. Listening to the voice we get to know him. This is a very private man, a sensualist living happily within his narrow milieu with no desire for adventure or for intimacy. Socially he exhibits the casual tolerance of one who cares nothing for the dramas of others. We recognise his core characteristic: while he will lie about some things, he will not lie about his feelings. Now there is a word for this very modern hero as there was not then. Meursault is the epitome of 'cool'.

Meursault's refusal to play society's games will cost him his life. Caught in the fringe of a friend's drama, in a strange, dissociated moment he shoots an Arab. Earlier the Arab had wounded the friend; he drew a knife; Meursault did not 'form an intention' to kill him, and shooting an Arab was not much of an offence in French Algeria anyway. We expect him to get off. Instead he is sentenced to be guillotined, not because he shot the Arab but because his behaviour over those few days comes to the court's attention and enrages opinion against him: he went swimming, picked up a girl, watched a Fernandel film—and he had not wept at his mother's funeral. The Prosecuting Counsel sums up the offence: 'I accuse this man of burying his mother like a heartless criminal.'

After the sentence we wait with Meursault in his condemned cell, and through that long wait learn the obscenity of a state's scheduled doing to death of a young man who loves the sea, the sun, his girl's mouth and breasts. Nonetheless, the second half of *The Outsider* steadily loses the electric intensity of the first because Camus' voice progressively displaces Meursault's as he manoeuvres his character's acceptance of the 'benign indifference of the universe' which lies at the heart of Camus' absurdist philosophy. What begins as a novel transforms into a philosophical tract. Unwillingly, we begin to notice how very contrived the story is, for all the plangency of the narrating voice, and that it is enacted within a white space, a political void. Despite that convenient Arab, the complex racial politics of colonial Algeria are simply absent.

Bernhard Schlink gives his narrator Michael Berg his own birth-year: 1944. The novel's context is the struggle of the post-Nazi generation of Germans to come to terms with their country's Nazi past. Like Camus' it pivots on a court case: one of the 'concentration camp trials' launched in the early sixties to purge Germany of that past, and to punish a handful of the Nazis living complacently within the new state. Berg is a law student. The trials are for him a personal crusade: he and his companions of the 'clean' generation have made themselves connoisseurs of Nazi atrocities so they can be hurled like javelins against parents who had shamefully, unforgivably accommodated the Nazi régime. Berg's father had in fact shown courage in a small matter and lost his academic job over it, but his son remains remorselessly punitive. Michael is avid for justice and the purging of collective guilt by the exemplary punishment of the few—an ambition abruptly blunted when he finds one of those few to be a woman called Hanna Schmitz, once his lover, and whom he loves still.

For the outsider the distinctive horror of the Holocaust is that supremely evil things were done deliberately, systematically, and over years. For ordinary Germans the deepest horror, the most profound existential dismay, attaches not to the ideologues who conceived and planned the Final Solution, but to the ordinary men and women who executed those plans. No one who has read much Holocaust material could undervalue the human adaptability that enabled some individuals to survive the hideous conditions of the concentration camps. Nor could readers doubt the sinister potential of that human capability, as they watch men and women initially disgusted by the brutalisation and slaughter of defenceless civilians grow accustomed to doing what they were assured was their duty, and some to enjoy it. Bernhard Schlink is haunted by the question that haunts his generation: 'If the Nazis had been monsters, we would not have a problem. We would be here, and they would be out there. It is because they are not monsters that what happened is so challenging for us, and so frightening.'

Schlink accepts the challenge and explores the fear by creating a woman who is capable of inspiring love and who is not a monster—but who has performed monstrous acts. We first meet Hanna

Schmitz when she is briskly kind to the schoolboy Berg, whom she then, almost as briskly, seduces. They enjoy a secret, highly erotic affair, during which Hanna's physical being becomes as vivid and seductive to us as it is to infatuated Michael. Like him, we are disturbed by her occasional moodiness; like him we are powerfully attracted by her independence, her toughness, her weary humour. Then, without warning, Hanna leaves town—the boy thinks because he silently repudiated his mature working-class mistress on encountering her when he was with school friends. We share his self-hatred, and his desolation.

Michael is part-recovered from her loss and his own guilt when he sees Hanna Schmitz in the dock. Along with four co-defendants she is accused of having been an SS guard at Auschwitz and at a satellite camp over the last two years of the war, with all that implies of licensed brutality. The five women also stand accused of a specific atrocity: that in the last stage of the war when they were driving their prisoners westwards through the snow they left several hundred women prisoners to burn to death inside a locked church.

Hanna's appearance in the courtroom exposes not only her own but Michael's secret history. This woman who has imprinted herself upon his young senses, this woman whose taste and textures he will pursue in all his later sexual alliances, had been a concentration-camp guard before he knew her, and, it seems, an unusually committed one. His most immediate anguish is personal: like any jealous lover he is forced into sickening revisions of every fragrant memory. Hanna had been imperious in bed and out of it; she had exacted obedience, sometimes cruelly. A mature woman's natural assumption of authority over an adolescent lover—or an addiction to the taste of power? In one bewildering eruption of rage she struck him across the face with a belt. The buckle cut his lip; she collapsed in tears; they made up; afterwards she was tender. Was this a glimpse of Hanna the guard? Tender love names, tender love games, are retrospectively tainted by terrible suspicions. Hanna had imposed a ritual on their lovemaking: first Michael would read to her, then they would bathe each other, then they would make love. In the courtroom he learns that it was Hanna's practice in the camp to select frail young girls for her personal service, not for sexual play, but so that they would read to her. Her favour preserved them for a month or more, but when it was time for a new intake she would send her pet to the gas, and choose another. Did she also bathe them, did she make them bathe her, in the obscene intimacies of absolute power? Had she acquired Michael, scooped up so casually, primarily as a reader, not a lover at all—a toy discarded as easily as she discarded those doomed girls? Small puzzles resolve into one larger one: had this woman who had opened him like a flower, who had suffused his being, loved him at all? And even if she had—how could he have loved a woman who had done what she had done?

Turgenev has one of his percipient old women say: 'The heart of another is a dark forest.' With his usual sanguine audacity he has her say it not of some gnarled stranger but of the luminously candid young woman she has tended since birth. It is in that dark forest that Michael loses himself—a forest like those which have enclosed us all at some time or another, but thicker, darker and more dreadful. Hanna, whose central charm has been her solidity, has betrayed him in the worst, most destabilising kind of way, by being other than the person he had thought her to be.

But is she indeed so different? As he listens to the testimony he discovers another of Hanna's secrets. She is illiterate, and deeply ashamed of it. The knowledge forces him to yet more painful revisions of their shared past: her passion for being read to, her naively intense engagement with fictional characters, her wistful respect for learning, her strange ignorance of the world are now explained. He also realises that she left him and his city so precipitously not because he had wounded her but because she had been offered a promotion which would have exposed her shame. Instead she chose to flee. Her leaving was not his fault at all. The fact of Hanna's illiteracy also has implications for her trial: she volunteered for the SS not through ideological inclination, but again to avoid promotion; she could not have written the report used to establish her primary responsibility for the events of the night of the fire. She accepted the false imputation because she is more ashamed of her illiteracy than of the murders in the church.

Despite his new knowledge, despite the multiple revisions of their shared past, Hanna remains enigmatic. Michael stares at the tendrils curling at the nape of her neck as he listens to what she and her fellow guards routinely did to the starved and helpless women in their charge. Yet in the dock she is his Hanna still: brave, imperious, energetic. She is urgent in her desire to make her listeners grasp the confusion of that chaotic night, to understand that someone had to take responsibility when all the guards save a handful of women were dead, wounded or fled. (This is a night of air-raids. The church is burning because of an allied bomb. The nice apportioning of guilt is never easy.) She seems to have not the least awareness of the criminality of her act, only of her duty. Of the desperate women screaming in the church she says: 'We had to guard them and not let them escape.' This is the standard Nazi defence of 'I was only obeying orders'—but Hanna is making it in good faith.

So the court staggers towards judgment. Precise degrees of guilt, in this as in most Holocaust cases, cannot be established because the events themselves, given the confused, contradictory and fragmentary nature of the evidence, cannot be accurately reconstructed, nor individuals securely identified. Hanna, defeated in her attempt to make the court acknowledge the coerciveness of her situation, turns to what will become her central question: if she has indeed done wrong, if her devotion of duty has indeed misled her, when did she take the fatal step? At what precise point ought she have acted differently? She is passionately concerned. She yearns for enlightenment from these wise men. She asks the judge directly. And he cannot answer her.

Hanna's fellow-accused have no interest in truth: they are lying to save their skins. The judge can hear only what is legally pertinent, not what is humanly true. The court, misled by her self-exonerating co-defendants, alienated by her interventions, and ignorant of her inability to read and what that might explain about both her earlier actions and her conduct in court, sentences Hanna to life imprisonment. Her more canny co-defendants, at least equally guilty, escape with lighter sentences.

The court punishes Hanna as the court punished Meursault: for a failure to comply with conventional expectations. Like Meursault she is a solitary. She left her family and Romania at sixteen; thereafter she has been on her own. She changes cities and jobs frequently; she has no friends or institutional ties; she has had minimal opportunity for reflection and social illumination. With the war she takes a job in the Siemens factory; at twenty-two she joins the SS not through ambition but to keep her pathetic secret. Beyond the random readings exacted from Michael and her girl-slaves her only education has come from the chaotic world of the cinema. Belatedly we realise that Hanna is emotionally illiterate, too, that she lacks emotional insight, that she is touchy and aggressive, because she is unpractised in tenderness. Her illiteracy is at once a sign and a reflex of her social isolation.

The trial also reveals Hanna as possessing the secondary virtues so valued in the Germany of her time: she is conscientious, disciplined, responsible. On the night of the fire she takes her duty to be to keep the exhausted, frail women in her charge under restraint—even as they writhe in the flames. She sees her victims as objects, not people. Have those secondary virtues, together with the cluster of consequences of her concealed illiteracy, led her, step by stumbling step, to commit a vile crime? At what is to be their last meeting, in oblique explanation of her actions, she says to Michael: 'I have always had the feeling that no one understood me anyway, that no one knew who I was and what made me do this and that. And you know, when no one understands you, then no one can call you to account'—except, as she discovered in the long solitude of prison, the murdered dead.

Critics have complained that the 'concealed illiteracy' strand is too exiguous to sustain its burden in the narrative. I cannot grant that. In life people nurture secret shames, so why not in fiction too? More serious is the claim that the invocation of her illiteracy has the effect of exonerating Hanna. It is true that her social isolation is presented as leaving her morally inept. For a moment we might be tempted to judge her a victim, to conclude that her upbringing or the lack of it has been her downfall. But only for a moment. After all, many of the people involved in the Nazi murder machine participated for private rather than ideological reasons, and had been deprived of an 'adequate' moral education. Hanna could stand for all those other members of the German nation who abdicated individual moral responsibility to continue punctual, dutiful and obedient, so making themselves murderers. Her illiteracy might help explain her inability to recognise those desperate women as fellow humans, but it does not mitigate murder. There is no miscarriage of justice in Hanna's courtroom, only of equity: her co-defendants get off too lightly. Courts are often inequitable, and human justice is never absolute: it is an aspiration, not a condition, and always less than perfect. As for Hanna's sentence—what would be an adequate retribution for the murder of innocents?

Initially it seems that Hanna herself does not accept her guilt: at her sentencing she appears in what the outraged court takes to be an SS uniform—black suit, white shirt, black tie. A defiant re-presentation of her past self, a refusal to admit her crime—or accident, a further manifestation of her innocence before a world she has never been educated to understand, much less manipulate? Here as elsewhere Schlink grants us the beneficence of uninterpreted action. Only one thing is clear: the Hanna who leaves the courtroom, with a look 'proud, wounded, lost, and infinitely tired', is not contrite.

Contrition comes later. It is part of Schlink's genius that we must infer Hanna's moral transformation, the dramatic core of the book, with Hanna herself vanished from our sight. The prison governor tells us that Hanna has lived in the gaol 'as if in a convent', 'in a sort of meditation'. After years she teaches herself to read (we recognise her adamantine resolution), using her new skill to read intensively and, as far as we can tell, almost exclusively in concentration camp literature. There is a paradox concealed in the book's title. It is the illiterate Hanna who becomes The Reader; she who uses her reading to comprehend the world and her own actions within it. She uses that hard-won literacy to examine the process that led her to her crimes, to comprehend the humanity of the individuals she sent to their deaths, and to do penance. We must assume that she has reached her goal when, after eighteen years of imprisonment, she petitions for release. She believes she has expiated her guilt; that she may live in the world again.

Hanna also seeks recognition of her atonement from the one survivor of the fire. It is refused. Nothing can erase her action, and as her living victim says, absolution is not in the gift of the living: it lies with the wronged and speechless dead. Nonetheless, by the close of her story we are persuaded that Hanna has come to understand the nature of her crime and has done penance for it. In this flawed world there can be no better outcome than that.

As for Michael—there are derelictions less dangerous but more subtle than Hanna's. Michael takes pride in being morally rigorous. He is aware of the divergence between intentions and behaviour—'often enough in my life I have done things I have not decided to do.'

But his characteristic failure is not of acting unwisely, but of failing to act at all. Realising Hanna's illiteracy, realising that she could not have written the report that damns her, he decides to deny her tacit decision for silence and to warn the judge of the potential miscarriage of justice. He visits the judge. But when the judge assumes his visit to be no more than a social call by an ambitious young student, Michael fails to mention Hanna. That silence condemns her to life imprisonment. And when Hanna's trial persuades him of the law's failure to render perfect justice (with no reference to his own part in that failure), he retreats from the challenge of legal practice to opt for a life of research—into, as it happens, the deformed role of law within the Third Reich, where the divorce between law, justice and morality was absolute.

His personal life follows a similar pattern of self-protective evasion. A marriage proves less than satisfactory; he leaves it, abandoning a loved daughter. He knows the irreparable damage done by abandonment. He sees Hanna in court, she sees him—but he allows eight years to pass before he contacts her, and then keeps a careful distance, sending her cassettes of his voice reading the words he had read to her before. He speaks not a word of his own. If this is compassion, it is handled with very long tongs. Hanna learns to write; she writes to him; he writes not a word in reply. Surely this is cruelty? And then, with her release likely, and knowing he ought to visit her, he postpones the visit for months. He does not want her free. He wants his Listener where she is, accessible for his private uses, securely locked away from his meagre, orderly, comfortable life. We realise that this scrupulous fellow is a natural conformist, sensitive to guilt, choosing withdrawal, always avoiding conflict. He knows his tendency to betrayal by silence. He is less aware of his talent for accommodation. In that accommodation he stands as parable for the generation of Germans who took the easy way within Hitler's Reich, repudiating responsibility for what was being done, tucking guilt and doubt away, clinging to the rhythms of their own safe lives—the generation he has condemned so glibly.

In court Michael noted how quickly horror at the descriptions of atrocities numbed into acceptance—another manifestation of that Janus-faced human virtue, adaptability. He knows his own capacity for feeling has been numbed, not least from the sequence of blows Hanna has dealt him. That indifference will have fatal consequences. Hanna believes that, having expiated her guilt, she will be able to return to the world, but when she sees the change in Michael's face as he approaches across the grass, she knows she has become repellent to him too, and that the world has no place for her. It is a major failure of that most personal of moralities, love. Being Hanna, she takes decisive action.

Not long before I read *The Reader* I publicly opined that great literature could not be written out of the Holocaust: that the material was too various and too horrible and the moral complexities too great to be reduced to a tellable tale. Bernhard Schlink has proved me wrong. The story of Michael and Hanna is delicately, quietly told. In the course of its sober telling painful matters are exposed. We are forced to realise how intricately law, love, justice and morality are interwoven, how difficult it is to judge others justly when it is necessary that they be judged, how difficult it is to keep one's moral footing in an ordinarily complex world, how much more difficult in a world where steps taken in quasi-innocence lead to the abyss. As a member of Michael's generation Schlink has inherited the Holocaust too. He knows these things in his bones. What is remarkable is that he has the talent to transmute that knowledge into art, rendering the general and the political into the personal and individual with no simplification at all. We follow Michael in his random thoughts, his walks in the woods, his sad dreams, his unassuageable loneliness. We hear the pain of the boy still bright in the voice of the man. The younger Hanna etches herself into our memory, we trace the redemption of the older Hanna, we come to honour her, we mourn her death. And all this in a slender book of cool, clean prose, with no sense of effort at all.

1998

PLENTY HUMBUG

Academic conferences tend to be dull affairs because everyone present is a professional, and everyone plays by the rules. Writers' festivals aren't like that. What they are most like is improvised theatre, with everyone, on stage and off, an amateur. The formal topic for one particular session at the Sydney Writers' Festival a couple of years ago was Rosemary Neill's book *Whiteout: How Politics is Killing Black Australia*, but the real plot-line was how the three Aboriginal men on the panel would respond to their two white, female fellow-panellists and their largely white audience: whether some sufficiently reassuring representation of reconciliation would be acted out on the stage.

Rosemary, who spoke first, stuck resolutely to an account of her intentions in writing the book. Then the senior man spoke. He was about my age—a bit younger—and he had already lived about five biographies to my one. He had just been awarded a PhD in an academic career he began when he was over fifty. I have been at school since I was six.

In effect, he told us to leave him and his people alone: that we were ignorant, and dangerous in our ignorance. The second man said much the same thing rather more gently, adding that by contrast with his people we were horribly culturally impoverished. The third was a poet and, in the gracious way of poets, entrusted us with one of his poems, although it was pretty clear that he expected his few Aboriginal listeners to understand it better than we did. As the conscripted 'public intellectual' I spoke last; tried to extract some encouraging message out of all this; failed. These people had had enough not only of white malice, and white neglect. They had had enough of white interference, and even of white good will.

As we shuffled out into the rain a woman spoke to me. She said, with a kind of despairing self-disgust I recognised too well: 'I'm white, I'm middle class, I live here in Sydney, and I cannot bear what is happening. What can I do?' She was almost weeping. I muttered something about 'educating ourselves to be prepared for political action, if the time for action ever comes'. Even to me it sounded hollow. She has been on my conscience ever since. Now I would like to try to give her a better answer.

I am sure that this woman, like so many others, had been roused by the 'Bringing Them Home' report about the generations of Aboriginal children forcibly removed from their families to improve their chances in life. Whatever the defects of the report—under-researched because under-funded, selective, 'political'—there can be no doubt of the impact of its stories. Humans have a unique talent for stories: for telling them, for responding to them and for learning from them. They are the most economical technique we have for expanding experience. Sometimes we can have the sense that we are standing in quite different shoes; that we are experiencing the world from a different perspective. When the stories are true, that experience is a powerful incitement to action. The 'Bringing Them Home' stories were both true and almost unbearably poignant. So what did we do with the moral and political energies they roused?

What we mainly did was to try to classify muddled intentions and actions under large concepts to render them apt for moral judgment. That is, by and large, what public intellectuals are expected to do. One obvious example: we unleashed a controversy about the applicability of the term 'genocide' to what had been done here, and then about what adjectival qualifier—'cultural'? 'occasional'? 'sporadic'?—was appropriate. We also engaged in politics, trying to force a narrow and stubborn man to utter a two-syllable word, 'sorry', in public. We also kept reminding people of how internationally prized traditional Aboriginal culture was, directing attention towards dance, paintings, and the spiritual and intellectual sophistication of the 'Dreaming'. And we urged symbolic actions—walking across bridges, signing 'sorry' books, because doing those things were signs, however inadequate, of the sincerity of our hearts.

They were good things to do, and I am sure the Sydney woman had done them. But meanwhile she was hearing other stories, or fragments of stories; sometimes no more than snapshots of action. They came in the form of radio or newspaper reports from places with names she had never heard, and they told of the neglect or the physical and sexual abuse of children, of the beating and killing of women, of plagues of adolescent suicides, of suicidal substance-abuse with alcohol, drugs, petrol and solvents being used as if there were no tomorrow. They came like lightning flashes illuminating a Boschian landscape we did not recognise at all.

There is a demoralising condition psychologists call 'cognitive dissonance', when two incompatible ideas struggle to co-exist in one mind. I think we intellectuals set my woman and others like her up for it. I had the sense right through that time that we were declaiming with our backs turned to the desperate, disintegrating societies behind us, in part because we were entranced by our own discourse, in part because we were persuaded it mattered, in part because we were stricken by realising what our flourishing had cost them, but I think most because we knew ourselves to be incompetent to understand why these things were happening, save in the broadest post-colonial theoretical terms—'dispossession', 'impoverishment', 'despair'—which generalities somehow failed to grip the terrible realities we were looking at.

I know criticism is easy, especially for someone whose preferred position is on the sidelines. So I want to look at three lightning-flash scenes and to hold the light steady so we might draw closer to what is going on. Not Redfern, because Redfern is a special case drenched with symbolic importance. (I refer you to Gillian Cowlishaw's work for refracted light on Redfern.) My focus will be on two fringe camps and one 'remote community', because it is those kinds of settlements whites most readily think of when we think of 'Aborigines' rather than the seventy percent of people of Aboriginal descent who now live in the towns and cities, and because it is from places like these that the lightning-flash reports most often come.

First to push aside a couple of words that persistently block our attempts to grasp what is going on, beginning with the word 'community'. 'Community'. In our culture it generates a rosy glow, conjuring a cluster of families spilling in and out of each others' houses, looking after each others' kids, sharing values: a little commonwealth.

Aboriginal 'communities' are not like that. Most began as arbitrary agglomerations of tribes, often hostile to one another, rounded up and dumped down to live cheek by jowl on alien land, or worse, on land belonging to one group, so the interlopers were condemned to a chronic state of trespass, and the traditional owners to chronic grievance. Even where a people were settled on their own land, the very process of settling deformed traditional practices, traditional relationships. If 'community' evokes for us notions of expansive egalitarianism, in most Aboriginal 'communities' family remains the primary, visceral loyalty, and a major stumbling-block in the way of our democratic schemes for their improvement. In a few cases these artificial agglomerations have been hammered on the anvil of 'the colonial experience' into true communities, Aboriginal style, so we need permanent inverted commas around that word 'community'. In every case, we have to establish just what it means.

The second word is 'culture'. When we speak of 'traditional Aboriginal culture', we either think in 'high-culture' terms of dance, visual arts and so on, or, if our usage is slightly more anthropologised, we evoke a vision of a 'sharing' culture, which in these new-age days slides easily towards a notion of a 'caring' culture. We need to remember that 'sharing cultures' are moral economies designed to manage scarcity. Of necessity, they are tough on their members. You must share with some, you must not share with others. They also leave 'outsiders' outside.

I use the word 'culture' to mean the system of meanings that sustains a particular group at a particular time regarding their expectations of themselves and each other, a dynamic system of shared meanings through which we communicate with our own. Because cultural meanings are rarely made explicit, understanding another culture's meanings is and always will be a hazardous enterprise. There is a sentimental notion abroad that we humans, skin-colour and costume aside, are all the same under the skin. I blame it on that 1950s collection of photographs titled 'The Family of Man'—gorgeous babies, grinning ancients, heart-stoppingly beautiful children, great hats, and that cute Peruvian boy playing the flute on the cover. It found its way into every household, even my parents'. But it isn't true. We are not the same. We are different. That is our burden, and our glory.

For me, the most compelling theme in our multi-level national history is our failure to grasp the continuing cultural differences between the descendants of the original Australians and the rest of us.

The first lightning-flash illuminates one such difference: what can look to us to be a terrifying Aboriginal propensity for unembarrassed, public, verbal and/or physical violence.

Just as each culture has its own concept of what constitutes masculine courage or feminine grace, so each culture is differently habituated to inflicting and enduring violence. Most of us have not suffered physical assault since primary school, and when we see public violence it is usually decently clad in the brief garments of sport. When it is not, we call the cops to do the authorised violence necessary to put a stop to it.

In *Dancing with Strangers*, my history of what happened in Australia in the first few years after 1788, I counterpoised what the British saw as wild, out-of-control Aboriginal violence—bashings, spearings, all-in battles—against what Aboriginal Australians saw as wild, out-of-control British violence—hangings, shacklings, floggings. Each culture drew its own lines to separate socially sanctioned from unauthorised and therefore illegal violence. Drawing the lines differently, they persistently got each other wrong, as when Phillip fetched up getting himself speared at what he thought was a reconciliation party—which indeed it was, in its way.

David Collins, Judge Advocate to the new colony and therefore a man with a professional interest in keeping the King's peace, spotted the inter-cultural problem early:

> An inhabitant of Port Jackson is seldom seen, even in the populous town of Sydney, without his spear, his throwing-stick, or his club. His spear is his defense against enemies. It is the weapon which he uses to punish aggression and revenge insult. It is even the instrument with which he corrects his wife in the last extreme; for in their passion, or perhaps oftener in a fit of jealousy, they scruple not to inflict death…
>
> It is easy to perceive what effect this must have upon their

> minds. They become familiarised to wounds, blood, and death; and, repeatedly involved in skirmishes and dangers, the native fears not death in his own person, and is consequently careless of inflicting it on others.

For an Aboriginal man at the time of contact, defence of rights and enforcement of law lay with his own person. That cultural understanding was to have large consequences on ongoing social relations between black and white.

I offer a description of one violent moment from a postcolonial Aboriginal 'community', this one remarkable because it was created not by whites but independently, indeed illegally, by Aborigines: the Darwin fringe-camp Basil Sansom immortalised as *The Camp at Wallaby Cross.* Aboriginal entrepreneurs developed the camp as a safe house for Aboriginal stockmen and mission people come to the city to drink their accumulated back-pay or pension cheques. It functioned as a hostel for transient binge-drinkers on a base of more permanent members-by-choice. Sansom is my kind of anthropologist because he pulls us into close-up on a particular incident, and then tries to work out what is going on. From his marvellous book I choose one event. And yes, I know the dangers of the misuse of material like this.

The Scene. It is late morning. We are inside the camp. A big man, a hundred-plus kilos, is beating a woman, his current wife, before a large group of people, who are watching but making no attempt to intervene. The woman lies on the ground, unresisting; he is hitting her with a metre-long piece of wood and shouting abuse as he hits her. He hits her eight times, then walks away, continuing to proclaim his grievances. He has been drinking, but he is not drunk. The man's daughter then attacks the woman, pummelling her; the woman moans; the man comes back, kicks her in the face four times, walks away still shouting; the girl pummels the woman again. Then the man picks up an axe, a woman in the crowd calls imperiously for him to put it down, he does so, walks away; the daughter pummels the woman, walks away; the woman lies sobbing; the watching people disperse. It is over.

This scene has a special interest for me because it eerily echoes the scene Baneelon staged before Governor Phillip when, after publicly proclaiming both his grievances and his murderous intentions (so collecting an anxious cloud of British witnesses), he snatched up a weapon and attacked a young woman who made not the least attempt to protect herself before a group of silent watchers who made no attempt to intervene. And when Phillip's men grabbed him, Baneelon was ecstatic with rage.

Phillip was disgusted by what Baneelon did that day, as we are with this scene. Nonetheless, and exactly because cherished cultural values are so directly outraged—large man beating small woman, violence inflicted on an unresisting victim, no intervention by onlookers—it is essential that we understand what is happening from the participants' point of view. Sansom diagnosed the scene as an act of moral violence: in other words, of authorised justice, with the grievance publicly proclaimed, the punishment publicly inflicted and then publicly terminated: when the man picks up the axe the watching woman calls in effect 'Hold! Enough!' And he stops. If he hadn't, Sansom believes that silent audience—that jury—would have intervened.

Furthermore, Sansom believes that had the man been drunk, the people of the drinkers' camp at Wallaby Cross would have intervened earlier. There seems to have been a general view among Aborigines (a view that now seems to be changing) that drunks aren't responsible for what they do—a belief that seethes with uncomfortable implications. However, one implication is that you can't do proper justice when you are drunk. Therefore in my view there is no continuity between the socially-controlled moral violence we have just been watching, and the individual, uncontrolled, sometimes lethal violence we see in many Aboriginal communities today, most often inflicted by drunken men on women—with the 'community' (remember those quotation marks) too exhausted or too little concerned to intervene.

The camp at Wallaby Cross impresses me as a remarkable post-colonial Aboriginal creation: a community, this time without quotation marks, built out of the radical displacement and radical mixing of tribal groups. The camp also managed to tame that flamboyantly destructive introduced element, alcohol. The people at Wallaby Cross, drinkers themselves, held alcohol's potential to dissolve social bonds in check, and they did it on territory reconquered from the colonisers, or, more precisely, from the Darwin municipal council. The camp's enduring *raison d'etre* was to exist free from white control while still enjoying the white man's irresistible gifts of alcohol, radios, guitars, flash stockmen's gear, store provisions, tobacco. Sansom's tight focus on the particular and the actual lets us look deeper, past that initial shudder, to an unfamiliar but impressive form of community.

This brilliant colonial evolution from tradition depended on a small but secure economic base. Bonus capital might be injected into the community from outsiders' pay cheques, but its stability depended on the judicious deployment of the government pensions regularly paid to the old, to widows, and to mothers receiving child support. The recipients handed over their cheques to the camp organisers who were its *de facto* elders in return for protection, security and prestige; these elders of this invented community organised corroborees, even initiations out of their (highly irregular) use of government funding.

I don't know what happened when unemployment benefits came in. My guess is that the uncontrolled inflow of money to the young and strong would disrupt a moral economy based on the controlled redistribution of scarce resources. An experiment in social adaptation destroyed by benevolent intervention.

Another glimpse of a postcolonial agglomeration of indigenous people responding creatively to the devastations attending the white man's coming: this time the Warumungu from around Tennant Creek. They had had a hard time of it. Pastoralists had been thrusting into their arid country from the turn of the century, with all the usual brutalities. Then in 1934 gold was discovered, and in came the miners. A young anthropologist named Bill Stanner happened to be in the vicinity and describes the brand of European Civilisation the Warumungu had to try to deal with:

> A stretch of bush pockmarked with scattered shafts...little food, less water, almost no ready money; rough humpies and scores of hard customers with that worst of fevers, gold fever. I had to keep a gun hard by to guard my stores.

Stanner heard talk of the necessity of clearing the remaining Aborigines out of the way and shifting them to a stretch of country where despite having local guides he himself nearly died from lack of water. He therefore reported what was being planned to the only authorities he knew: his Research Council. Without result: as he says, with typical Stanneresque economy, 'the miners won and the Warumungu lost.' So Tennant Creek was born.

There is an alternative myth to explain this sudden blossoming of a town in the middle of a desert. En route to elsewhere a beer truck broke down; people came from nowhere and camped beside it, and Tennant Creek was born like Aphrodite from the foam. The myth has the usual substratum of truth: from its beginning Tennant Creek was a town of gargantuan drinkers.

The white town grew with the usual fringe of displaced Aborigines living in squalid camps around it: camps that C. D. Rowley described in the late sixties as 'among the worst on the continent'. Some families were still living on their home country as (largely unpaid) workers on cattle leases. Some came into town when the Federal Government began paying old age and widows' pensions in the late fifties, because those small payments opened a tiny window of choice. Others were abruptly tipped off their lands in the early seventies when equal pay for black and white stockmen came in—a decision taken elsewhere, for the usual mixed motives, and with no consultation with the people most affected—and they had to cram into the town camps too. Where else could they go? Soon there were ten camps containing sixteen different language groups. The Warumungu had been very thoroughly processed by 'the colonial process'.

Tennant Creek became famous for its wild Aboriginal drinkers, providing quite a few lightning flashes to astonish white Australia. Then in the mid-eighties something remarkable happened. A representative council emerged from those camps, we don't know how because it happened well out of white sight. Julalikari Council included representatives from all the camps and all the language groups, so breaking free from the crippling constrictions of clan and family loyalties and the conflicting traditional ownerships that continue to bedevil most Aboriginal politics today. It had only one purpose: to fight the effects of grog on the people.

Tennant Creek, population sixty percent white, forty percent black, was famous for its night scenes of drunken Aborigines surging out of the liquor outlets, brawling up and down the main street, smashing expensive windows, fighting, bleeding, sometimes dying on the pavements. So the Council organised a Night Patrol. Unpaid volunteers, most of them senior people, many of them women, all of them non-drinkers, went out at night in pairs, in a van or more often on foot, to collect drunks and to break up trouble before it could explode into violence. (Some senior members of the Night Patrol were putting in thirty hours a week.) The Council also staged 'morning-after' petty sessions in the different camps. Men who would take on white police without thinking twice blenched when they had to face the anger of the kin and neighbours they had monstered the night before. And note the innovation. These drunks were being held responsible for their action, and their families would not protect them from the formidable community punishment of public shaming.

Meanwhile the meat works and the mine had closed, white Tennant Creek had fallen on hard times, and local businessmen were dreaming of a tourist-led recovery. They didn't want those phantom tourists frightened off by mobs of all-too-real drunken Aborigines. In March 1994, they called a 'summit' on grog, with the title making their priorities plain: 'Tennant Creek, Tourism and Grog'.

Julalikari Council had been carrying its analysis further, from issues of misuse to issues of supply. Camps that had proclaimed themselves 'dry' were still being ringed by binge drinkers, with the drunks bringing their violence and their rage back into the home camp when the grog ran out, so at that first summit meeting the Julalikari Council moved to restrict the availability of alcohol in Tennant Creek, which is possible under Northern Territory law. They wanted a grog-free day (Thursday, pension-day), and for the rest of the week pub and takeaway hours to be restricted from noon until 8 p.m., with takeaways limited to six cans per person and the sale of wine casks prohibited. And (this was the rub) they wanted those restrictions to apply to everyone in Tennant Creek, black and white alike. They were asking for a social—indeed, given the power relations in the town, a political—revolution.

What happened next is told in a book written by Alexis Wright, an Aboriginal woman from the Gulf country called in by the Council to write the history of the struggle. She calls her book *Grog War*, because that is what it was. Initially it is a difficult book to read: Wright uses a kind of hand-held camera technique for reporting the two-year-long round of meetings between the Julalikari Council and the liquor interests before the Northern Territory Liquor Commission, with the rest of the town lined up barracking. There were some interesting re-alignments. Aboriginal and white drinkers united in opposition to the Council. So did Aboriginal and white progressives, seeing the right to drink as emblematic of Aboriginal enfranchisement. White Territorians knew it was their basic human right to drink what, when and where they chose: after all, it wasn't their fault that Abos couldn't handle the grog. Their solution was easy: let the blackfellas buy whatever grog they wanted as takeaway and then go back to the camps to drink it, just as they used to in the good old days of *de facto* curfew.

Tennant Creek publicans were playing a seriously hard game, suffused by a deep moral flush in defense of individual rights and what they insisted were legitimate commercial interests. They were defending life, liberty and the pursuit of profits: as liquor sellers they had both the right and the duty to provide a service and to profit from uncoerced commercial transactions. And these transactions were certainly uncoerced: they themselves had proved Aborigines were so desperate to buy alcohol they would buy under any conditions. They were also aggrieved by the necessity of competing with their fellow publicans for what threatened to be a diminished trade: that was anti-mate, anti-social, anti-Australian. As for the rest—once the Abos were out of the pub they weren't their problem. That was for the police, or the Night Patrol, or the government. Or someone.

Race relations in the town, always bad, were now vicious, so the Liquor Commissioner offered a concession: he was ready to introduce a special measure to the Anti-Discrimination Act and to restrict the availability of alcohol to Tennant Creek's Aborigines. The Council refused. Bloody-minded? You bet. Why not, after their history? But there was more than bloody-mindedness going on here.

A new sense of community was struggling to be born in a deeply, casually hostile environment. This is when Wright's close reporting of apparently futile exchanges matters. We watch as people wearily trade the same old slogans like punches; as these two people forced by history to live in proximity, find new ways to vex each other. (Both sides loathed the other one's conduct in court.) And as we listen, we identify a language problem. Both sides were using the same words, but they meant different things by them.

When the Julalikari Council people talked about 'the community' they meant 'all of the people living in this place'. Country, language, tribe had been remorselessly taken from them. Now they were making a new community out of what they had. They had consistently refused to abandon their own disruptive drinkers to some nether world of despair and rejection. Instead, night after night, through the years, they had gone out to gather them up, and bring them home. They had cared for some old white people camped near them in exactly the same way. They also knew the tight nexus between the financial interests of white suppliers, and the costs of alcohol dependence. They knew that down to the last bruised woman, the last hungry child. They also knew that when whites started talking loudly about their 'rights', Aborigines do well to watch their backs.

Grog War holds up a mirror in which we see reflected the Aboriginal experience of us. Reading it, I felt the terrible justice of the judgment on whites made to Bill Stanner by an old Aboriginal man after years spent trying to co-exist civilly with us: 'Very clever people; very hard people; plenty humbug.'

That is not the way we look to ourselves, but I think it is the way we still can look to them, however virtuous our intentions, however elevated our rhetoric—often because of its very elevation.

What happened at Tennant Creek? After two years of talk, and trials of different kinds of restrictions, the Council got most of what they wanted. The Town Council, which had previously opposed them, moved sleekly to take the credit, another familiar white strategy. And the majority of white residents, along with the majority of black residents, applauded the victory: their town was now a better place to live. The council's obstinacy had created a community that had not existed before: a community that transcended race boundaries. There was still division, but now it ran between irresponsible drinkers and suppliers, black and white—the publicans and the sinners—and the rest of the citizenry, white and black.

Of course it is not all roses. The obsessive drinking continues, though it is rather more orderly. The police and the Council work together well. There is what one of the Council warriors, a remarkable man called Dave Curtis (look him up on the internet) calls 'a modicum of racial harmony' where there had been none before. In this war the victories are small, and always precarious.

My last lightning-flash comes from a place called Curtin Springs, on the Lasseter Highway about 100 kilometres east of Uluru. There is a roadhouse there. It was opened in 1964 by a pastoralist who had taken up his lease only four years before, and who wanted to expand his meagre income by serving tourists on the thirsty drive to Uluru tourist country. His application for a liquor licence was passionately opposed by the three Aboriginal communities in the region, all of them, although officially 'dry', beset by alcohol, but the licence was granted anyway. So the licensee, who was not a bad fellow, arrived at a gentleman's agreement with the communities. All drinking would be done on the premises. There would be no takeaway sales. Then in 1988, with his income shrinking as tourism dropped off, he began to exercise his legal right to sell takeaway alcohol to Aborigines. He did, however, limit the sales to one carton of beer and one four-litre wine cask per person per day. Per person. The young men would come in from the settlements, drink, and then take themselves, their supplies and their drunkenness back to their 'dry' communities, and turn them into nightmares. Very clever people. Very hard people. Plenty humbug.

So the women of the besieged communities organised, withdrawing consent both from their traditional powerlessness and the new powerlessness imposed on them by white authorities. They fought with new weapons, holding public meetings; marching, painted and with banners, down empty roads with the cameras prearranged. And they talked, loud and clear, in public, like this Anangu woman before the Liquor Commissioner: 'We have been asking for years and years to close Curtin Springs down. I ask you could you not listen to us for once? We have lost a lot of our lads to drinking. We are not going to cry all the time.'

They were of course reminded that as citizens Aborigines had an equal right with whites to drink. But these women were speaking out of a concept of rights that went well beyond the individual, and they had the dreadful weight of experience behind them. So the Curtin Springs women reached past the local and further into the public sphere. They went after a 'special measure' exemption from the Anti-Discrimination Act, and finally they got it after, may I say, a woman commissioner had come into office. The roadhouse-keeper was forbidden to sell takeaway liquor to Anangu people.

Of course the destabilising thrusts have kept coming. Right now those same Anangu communities are tottering under a great upsurge in petrol sniffing. As I write this, Bob Collins has taken over the administration of Anangu-Pitjantjatjara lands further south, in response to a plea from the women, to try to get some action to combat it. Petrol sniffing is also resurgent among white kids in the Northern Territory, perhaps because they are realising they have almost no choices, either.

So now I think the three Aboriginal men in Sydney were right. I think we must wait on local Aboriginal initiatives, because only local Aboriginal initiatives are sufficiently informed by local knowledge of the particular historical experience and the particular balance of pressures and personalities in a particular place, at a particular time.

We will find the waiting hard. Like the Minister for Aboriginal Affairs, we 'naturally' favour clean, across-the-board solutions, and—like the Minister—we have a mighty urge to intervene. I think Aboriginal Australia has suffered enough from our impatient, or ignorant, or careless interventions—like the families tumbled off their country when equal wages came in, or Wallaby Cross, with unemployment relief disrupting that delicately calibrated moral economy. We will also have to learn to practise an unfamiliar virtue: to tolerate uncertainty. Understanding a profoundly different culture is a slow business, especially given the mistrust generated by a history of systematic injustice. It will be a slow road to enlightenment, with those 'Ah! Now I see!' moments mere stations along the way. We must no longer depend on a mix of sound-bite compilations and moral intuitions to form our judgments, nor the brief, blinding illuminations of lightning flashes, either. We need good, up-close, non-ideologised anthropologies of particular places, or the evolution of particular problems traced through time. There is already an abundance of marvellous studies buried in academic archives, like Maggie Brady's analysis of petrol sniffing, now a decade old, still utterly relevant, or David McKnight's angry, loving, informed account of what has happened from settlement to now on Mornington Island.

One part of the public intellectual's ill-defined job is to exhume those analyses and report them to the general public: to help them understand why particular communities have been brought to the pass they are in, so their plight becomes humanly intelligible to us, and not some blank crime of nature or history. We can't expect journalists to do that. Their concern is with the lightning-flash 'now'. We can't expect the researchers to do it, either. They have to report to their departmental employers, or to their peers, so their work will typically need translation for a general readership.

We will also have to decide to which voices we will listen, when there are so many voices, some opportunistic, some ideologised beyond recovery, some embittered beyond recall. As with any society, we will listen to the voices which command our respect: where we hear experience and intrepid reasoning informing speech and actions. I hear those qualities in Noel Pearson's voice: Pearson, whose intelligence and natural eloquence would have given him a national career, but who chose to turn back to his own Cape York mob, and to work for them; Pearson, who knows the odds. A few years ago he gave himself a fifty-fifty chance of doing what he knows must be done if destruction is to be averted. I also listen to Pearson because he makes me recognise my own areas of cultural blindnesses. These days I find myself coming to agree with him where I had disagreed before. I listen to Bob Collins, who happens to be white, because he, like Pearson, is locked into local circumstance; because, like Pearson, he is an effective hinge-man, responsive to local insights, yet capable of manipulating national authorities; and because his recognition of his moral duty goes beyond cultural difference to where our shared humanity resides.

And I will listen to the equivalents of Julalikari Council and the women of Curtin Springs. Toni Morrison once explained her deep pleasure in Greek tragedy by its family resemblance to the fierce battles fought between the claims of the individual, the family and the community among deracinated Afro-Americans. The women at Curtin Springs were impelled by external forces well beyond their control to make a Sophoclean choice: to jeopardise the lives of their beloved sons, husbands, brothers—to condemn them to the long, dangerous drive to Alice Springs to get the grog they could not live without; then to be alone in Alice, beyond the loving protection of their kin—in order to preserve the rest of their community. Any culture must honour the terrible clear-sightedness of that choice, and that they should have had the courage to discover choice at all in that apparently sealed and hopeless situation.

Alexis Wright used this quote from a white resident of Tennant Creek as the epigraph for her *Grog War*: 'I know what Aboriginal people do because I watch them from the top of the hill.'

I think we will need to draw much closer than that.

2004

DISPATCHES FROM THE HISTORY WARS

Reading Stuart Macintyre's *The History Wars* reveals the sole compensation for getting old: I discover I have been present at historical events. As a junior tutor in the History Department at Melbourne University I used to watch Manning Clark, wide-hatted, portentous, on his sombre visitations from his exile in Canberra, and noted the distinctive mix of irony and affection with which he was greeted. I also met Geoff Blainey when I was still a History undergraduate and he a postgraduate, usually off somewhere in Tasmania writing real history instead of only talking about it, as the rest of us were. In that rarified atmosphere he was a breath of home air, and I liked and trusted him immediately, as I continue to do. While I have disagreed with some of his analyses and many of his conclusions, I have never doubted his integrity. I have also been grateful, because he has shown me an Australia otherwise invisible to me. Where I would see only a ravaged landscape—gaunt paddocks, decaying fences, collapsed windmills—Blainey made me see the archaeology of human endeavour, the ambitions, triumphs and despairs, concealed within that starkness. He also made me see the drama of technological invention as men (they were mostly men) struggled to impose their will in this recalcitrant continent.

Later I began to hear bizarre tales of the Order of Lenin or some other shiny object possibly glimpsed beneath Clark's ample beard, and watched with regret as Blainey's laconic but passionate nationalism brought him into bruising conflict with most members of his home department over the contentious issue of the level and pace of Asian migration into this country. But mainly I got on with teaching and researching the history of quite other lands, and occasionally writing about them.

Now, having read *The History Wars*, I feel like Rip Van Winkle emerging blinking from my cave into a scene of carnage—walls down, trees upended, bodies tossed about—as events which I had taken for what might be called epiphenomena reveal themselves as manifestations of an epic struggle over what kind of story about its past Australia ought to be telling itself. Stuart Macintyre, Ernest Scott Professor of History at the University of Melbourne and a veteran of teaching, writing and administering Australian history, has set out to give us the long view of what has been going on in Australian history over these last decades. He identifies the recent fuss over Keith Windschuttle's *The Fabrication of Aboriginal History* as being powered by the same engine as an earlier, longer and more important battle waged for the nation's soul between the supporters of Manning Clark, and of Geoffrey Blainey. Macintyre cares about the battles because he believes that national-story-making-and-telling is properly the job of professional historians, and over a handful of pages he bravely, if not altogether wisely, tells us why.

He explains that history is not given, as people like John Howard think, but made. It is made by historians, who approach the historical record with certain hypotheses in mind, retrieve the relevant evidence through professionally approved procedures of historical research, make the necessary adjustments to the initial hypothesis, and then present their selected, retrieved facts in the form of a story: 'Of all [history's] devices, the narrative is the most compelling for it creates a sequence of factual events and connects them with a dramatic momentum that carries the history forward from starting point to conclusion.' He acknowledges that that is not how life is actually lived —'Life is lived in the present without the benefit of a grand narrator'—but the professional historian is empowered to narrate the past, presumably as grandly as he chooses, because 'it is the historian who enjoys the advantage of hindsight to select particular events and to arrange them into a coherent pattern. The facts do not exist prior to the interpretation that establishes their significance'.

There are historians, and I am one of them, who would object to this account. John Howard certainly would. But history's house has many mansions, and we would all agree that respect for the record, recognition of its inadequacies, and caution and candour in its interpretation are at the core of our discipline. There is, however, a peculiarity about the History Wars, at least in Macintyre's telling of them: they are being fought by only one side. Despite being under constant withering fire, the historians have got blamelessly on with their historians' duties, testing hypotheses against the records, steadfastly narrating the results.

That is not quite how it has looked to me. Anna Clark's illuminating contribution to *The History Wars* describes the savage battles over the teaching of history in schools, with at least two sides fiercely engaged, while Macintyre himself chose Paul Keating to launch his book, with predictably incendiary consequences, and declares his own sympathies with cheerful partisanship. Nor has overstatement been restricted to one side. Some of Windschuttle's opponents have come close to matching his casual attribution of disreputable motive, his freehand psychologising, his overheated ideologising. Even Robert Manne, angered by Windschuttle's extravagant and provocative claim that in the story of the empire, Tasmania was probably the place where 'the least indigenous blood of all was deliberately shed', riposted with an extravagant claim of his own: 'Ever since the 1830s, civilised opinion has regarded Tasmania as the site of one of the greatest tragedies in the history of British colonialism.' If that is true, 'civilised opinion' is, simply, wrong. British colonialism has contrived more than a few tragedies in its long history, many bloodier and more wilful than the piecemeal and partial destruction of the Tasmanians.

It is, however, true that historians working in Australia, including distinguished researchers into Aboriginal history, have not been actively engaged in the Windschuttle war, and those who have engaged have been directly attacked. In his *Fabrication* Windschuttle talks vaguely of an 'orthodox school', but his primary targets are Lloyd Robson, who is dead, Lyndall Ryan, who wrote her pioneering work for her PhD thirty years ago, and Henry Reynolds. Reynolds has been the primary target throughout, because he led the inquiry into black–white relations in this country, and because he has always made clear his hope that his academic work would have political and legal consequences—as it has, most obviously in the legal thinking behind the Mabo judgment.

Given the times, it is perhaps necessary to say that I have never met Henry Reynolds. But I have always admired him, because his passion for justice has existed alongside a scrupulous regard for the record, transparency of argument, and an extraordinary capacity for sustained research and lucid writing. He has also remained admirably urbane in the face of misrepresentation by friends and enemies alike. Because I admire Reynolds' work, I have to confess an initial impatience at the time and space given by serious people to 'the Windschuttle affair', which was so obvious a beat-up. Surely Reynolds had already dispatched such arguments? Reynolds, who knew the ambiguities, omissions and evasions of the colonial records as few others do, knew it was impossible to arrive at a strict count of the number of Australian Aborigines deliberately killed during the colonising process, much less the number lost to disease or malnutrition; that only a fraction of black killings would have any presence in white records. He knew that for us literate folk, Aboriginal folk memories would carry little weight. But he also recognised the legitimacy of his readers' desire for comparative figures on the killings perpetrated inside the different contact zones. So he chased down shadows, re-examined claims, scrutinised legal findings, pointed to the necessary approximations, and came up with estimates which he clearly labelled as estimates. By contrast Windschuttle, who appears to take colonial records as direct representation of actuality, produces a 'hard' figure for Tasmanian killings: a figure that sagged under criticism. In the conditions of the colonial encounter, with records sparse and local authorities few, weak and often self-serving, Windschuttle's law-court criteria for admissibility are simply inappropriate. As Shane Breen briskly puts it: 'As every historian except Windschuttle knows, no context, no history.'

Has the war been worth the blood? Judging from the increasingly sardonic turn of the 'letters to the editor', I have the unhappy sense that the most immediate consequence of the public battles has been increased public cynicism about the historical enterprise, its pretensions and its practitioners ('Just how many professors of history are there at the University of Melbourne?'). Yet—the Windschuttle volume was certainly having a wide effect. Within a couple of weeks of its publication I had been asked by four people, only one of them an academic and each on separate occasions, what I thought of Windschuttle's attack on my discipline and what I intended to do about it. These intelligent readers had been much impressed by Windschuttle's apparent scrupulosity, and by what they took to be his sterling empiricism. So—grudging the time—I read the volume to see what that sterling empiricism added up to, and reached my conclusions. I agreed with Manne; this was not genuine history, but 'plausible counterfeit coin'. I was nonetheless impressed by

Windschuttle's manifest sincerity, and disturbed by the referencing errors he uncovered. Wilful fabrications? No. We all know the witchcraft that afflicts even the simplest act of transcription, and the legion of poltergeists infesting the process of keeping text and references in lockstep from manuscript through redrafts to final publication. Nonetheless, Ryan's errors in particular seemed multiple and consequential, and cried out for explanation. Some of Windschuttle's critiques were compelling, and had to be answered; some were grotesque, and had to be demolished. So what was to be done?

The most active gladiators on the 'history' side (which was at no stage as well-organised as its opponents) have been political scientists and philosophers, along with academics of no clear disciplinary affiliation, a few journalists, and the occasional anthropologist. That should not surprise us. You can't do history on the opinion pages. Even Reynolds has never seemed quite at home there, although he has dutifully armoured up. Now historians have to thank the political scientist (and seasoned warrior) Robert Manne for marshalling their responses in the splendidly accessible volume he has edited, *Whitewash: On Keith Windschuttle's Fabrication of Aboriginal History* (which title, I have only now noticed, makes a neat jibe through a couple of tiny omissions).

From the outset Manne has believed the stakes to be high: that 'the future of Australia will be seriously affected by whether or not the Windschuttle view prevails' because 'if Windschuttle's account of the nature of the interactions between indigenous people and incomers is accepted, the hope for reconciliation is dead'. I have come to think he is right; that the challenge is simply too serious to be brushed aside. Unexpectedly, *Whitewash* is a delight. My one regret is that there is nothing in the title to tell us that this might be the best single volume on the colonisation of Tasmania we have to date. Stylistically it is bracingly pungent. A couple of anthropologically inclined archaeologists demolish Windschuttle's D.I.Y. anthropologising; a philosopher and a law professor combine forces to offer a subtle, useful analysis of the larger concepts illuminating the particular case. We hear a couple of indigenous voices, one simple and urgent, one sophisticated and equally urgent. There is a piece of intellectual trampolining by Dirk Moses which some people will enjoy, and a sober, fair-minded introduction from the editor.

And then there are the historians. One, a specialist in criminal justice, evaluates Windschuttle's idiosyncratic arithmetic. Lyndall Ryan reminds us how we worked thirty years ago—pencil-written notes, endless retypings—and demonstrates her errors to be few, explicable and trivial. Reliable Reynolds explores aboriginal words demonstrating attachment to land; Shane Breen traces present consequences. Cassandra Pybus offers a nuanced reading of that multiple man, George Augustus Robinson, correcting the Vivienne Rae-Ellis caricature which Windschuttle trusted because his political sympathies lay with the author. The evidence relating to particular 'massacres' in Tasmania and elsewhere is reassessed, and the deficiencies in the Windschuttle analyses exposed.

The jewel of the collection is the opening essay by James Boyce. Boyce presents a scrupulous, ruthless anatomising of Windschuttle's arguments, and a damming exposé of his occasionally weird research methodology, or, more correctly, his hunting-and-collecting techniques: for example, his tendency to rely on books with the heading 'Aborigines' in the indices, which accessible information is then elaborately processed while other less docile or more reticent sources are ignored. Windschuttle's 'detail', so persuasive to the novice, is demonstrated to be radically selective and radically decontexted. Against Windschuttle reconstructions Boyce brings deep local knowledge derived from the critical analysis of the full range of available documentation. If you want to read some passages of fine, informed history, read Boyce on 'The Competition for Game' and

'The Competition for Land'. It is a thrilling performance. If the discipline in Tasmania can produce historians of this calibre, it is in the very best of hands.

Boyce demonstrates decisively that good history drives out bad. He, along with the other locals in this volume, has also persuaded me out of an old prejudice. I was so weary of the contest over which fable should be adopted as the national story I was beginning to think that people should be forbidden to work on the history of their own country: that 'Australian History' ought be handed over to, say, Ethiopians, or Serbs. This volume has persuaded me that a focussed passion for a land can—if expressed within the rules of the discipline—deepen understanding.

Keith Windschuttle is a warrior. His primary object is not the better understanding of what went on between the indigenous population and incomers in the early years of settlement in Tasmania, but to collect the scalps of a (vaguely-defined) tribe of historians he has marked as the enemy, and who he believes have wilfully deceived the Australian public regarding the character both of our first settlers and of the people they encountered. He makes his unabashed present-mindedness explicit in the ferocious denunciations of his final chapter. Unsurprisingly, he is at his most implausible in his representation of the native Tasmanians, who lurk at the periphery of civilised settlement like escapees from a Swiftian nightmare, natural-born criminals so maladapted to their environment that their survival for 35,000 years could rationally be explained only by a rather extended period of good luck.

The discipline of history demands rigorous self-criticism, a patient, even attentiveness, and a practised tolerance for uncertainty. It also requires that pleasure be taken in the epistemological problems which attend the attempt to recover the density of a past actuality from its residual traces. These are not warrior virtues. Windschuttle detests ambiguity, and is blind to epistemological problems, instead applying forensic modes of interrogation simply inappropriate to such delicate material. His ideological excitation adds its own airy dimension. For all the sound and the fury, Windschuttle is weaving the wind.

If for Windschuttle 'history' is a contemporary contest over the stories to be told about the national past, Macintyre, chief of a very different tribe, who also relishes the battle metaphor, comes close to agreeing with him. Must history really be a clash between opposed epics? Or might it be something quite different—ambiguous, contestable, potentially inclusive? Humans are good at story-making, and the narratising impulse is powerful in every one of us. We imagine our lives as we live them, even as we endure painful periods of radical revision. Social groups are held together through shared stories that sustain the preferred vision of the individual, of the group and of those others who exist beyond the group, defining its boundaries. But if our story-making is personally and socially necessary, its consequences are protean, and some can be malign. We know this. We have watched the recent deformations of story and history in the efflorescence of national and tribal myths for which men, women and children have died.

The stories made from history always have political implications, but that does not constitute their authority over us. History helps us to know who we humans are, and of what we are capable. It also reminds us that, however complicated the situation, however apparently compelling the circumstances, there is always space for choice: that the individual conscience is our first, last and only refuge. The current politically motivated simplifications can only impede the development of our individual analytic capacities and a reliable sense of social responsibility. Historians have a special duty: to resist opportunistic falsification of the precious record of past experience, from whatever quarter the deforming impulse might come.

Our present condition is the consequence of everything we have been, and everything we have done. Therefore our history is and must be multiple. As for methodology: here are some words from a hero of mine, the very political historian E. P. Thompson, from his 'Agenda for Radical History': 'Radical history demands the most exacting standards of the historical discipline. Radical history must be good history. It must be as good as history can be.'

2003

BUILDING TREBLINKA

Elsternwick is the prototypical Melbourne leafy suburb, full of lawn sprinklers, wrens squabbling in hydrangeas, the distant whoosh of cars. The houses are ample and some of them handsome, and the shopping centre is a clean, well-lighted place with the smell of the sea about it. Shopkeepers greet their customers by name and chase them with forgotten parcels; matrons accost pram-wheeling mothers to interrogate them on the care and feeding of their startled babies. Along with its adjoining suburbs of Caulfield and St Kilda it is the heartland of Melbourne's large Jewish community.

Just off the shopping centre is a short, bald street which begins with a Jewish cake shop and ends with a jubilantly noisy school for Jewish children. Halfway along its length is the Jewish Holocaust Museum. Locals say that Melbourne has the largest community of Holocaust survivors in any city outside Israel, some say more than Tel Aviv. The museum is the creation of some of those survivors. They raised the money to build it, they supplied most of the exhibits, now they staff it.

The museum is housed in a narrow two-storey building of stuccoed brick. Three electric candles burn on each side of its heavy wooden doors in commemoration of the murdered six million, and the writing on the discreet brass name-plate is in both Hebrew and English. Inside, among the guides, the language is quickfire Yiddish or Polish (Melbourne is a largely Polish city; the Hungarians went to Sydney) with the occasional German phrase tossed in, largely, as far as I could tell, for comic effect. Most of the upstairs space is occupied by an auditorium with a screen that lights up to reveal a map of the concentration camps, the work and holding camps picked out in red, the extermination camps marked by artfully flickering candle flames. A tiny coffee annexe for the staff is tucked in at the head of the stairs. Downstairs there is a small reception area—a desk, a few chairs, a few pegs for coats—a reference library, and the exhibition hall. It is here that the buses come with students from Melbourne secondary schools for their two-hour tours.

The museum's administrative section occupies a dishevelled suburban house next door. There is a great deal of coming and going across the scorched lawn, and inside all the doors, including the bathroom door, stand open. Abandoned coffee mugs roll in corners, photographs spill over tables, papers drift from chairs. The place looks pillaged, as if its occupants have been arrested, or have fled. The volunteer staff, dashing about with their armfuls of documents and sheaves of files between the ringing telephones, seem untroubled by my fantasies.

The exhibition hall is the core of the museum. It contains photographs: the ones we have come to know, and others not seen before but instantly recognisable as 'Holocaust photographs'—a boy spooning soup into his small sister's stretched mouth, pale, dark-eyed children in snow among birch trees, a press of people with bundles and baskets climbing into a train, with a tall young man with a farm-boy face under his cap and trailing a rifle standing nonchalantly behind them. There are photographs from Warsaw and Lodz, from Auschwitz, Belsen and Buchenwald. The school children shepherded through the museum are told that their guides are survivors of such places, but no more than that: the guides have agreed not to speak of their individual experiences. I am not sure how far the children grasp what they are being told—that the dapper elderly people talking to them could have been in any one of the photographs they are looking at—although one quiet woman turns her face away as she tells me that every time she talks to a group she feels herself naked and humiliated once again. She tells me this standing beside a photograph of three young Jewish girls, each with a lovely tumble of thick dark hair. They are naked. They look at the camera, their arms are at their sides. They have been ordered to stand like that. What do adolescent boys, what do adolescent girls, make of the photograph? The guide says that sometimes they laugh. She shrugs, sadly: do I think they will remember it later, when they are older, and not laugh?

The photographs snake around the walls in the usual sequence, from well-muscled Jewish cycling clubs with big moustaches and grins, soccer teams and marriages and scenes of shtetl life, through famine and corpses in the ghettoes, brutalisation and murder in the camps, to end with the heroes of the Warsaw Uprising and a parade of Righteous Gentiles. Glass cases follow the same route at hip level and in minor key, displaying small personal things rescued from the catastrophic narrative unfolding above them: things tucked into the single suitcase for the long journey to Australia. One small, very elegant man leads me to the case which holds his personal treasures: coins from the Lodz ghetto, some blotchy personal papers. He seems to look at them proudly, even fondly, but I do not know what he really feels. Like the striped prisoner's shirt displayed in the hallway, these coins, ragged yellow stars and near-indecipherable documents are not memorabilia, but the mesmerising trophies of an ineradicable, wholly desecrated past.

One corner of the display room has been used to create a

diorama: a cremation oven and a line of ragged prisoners painted on the wall, a near-to-life-size puppet in striped garments hanging on the wire in front of our faces. It is very dark in that corner, and the photographs of the patient queues and the skull faces and the well-fed men with whips and overcoats press closely at your back. It is difficult to understand how these living men and women, equable, tirelessly hospitable, can bear to turn from the sunlit street through the narrow door into the still grey air of their past. For an outsider the effect of threading these cramped alleys, these horrors so artfully deployed in so small a space, is a cumulative claustrophobia that leaves you quivering on the edge of panic.

It is therefore initially a relief to turn from the wall exhibits to the larger, lighter space in the middle of the room: a space occupied by an elaborate, three-dimensional model of the extermination camp at Treblinka.

'Treblinka'. It is a pretty, tinkling sound, conjuring mountain villages, toboggans, children's laughter in frosty air. In fact the land around Treblinka is flat and sandy. Pines grow well there, but there are very few birds. The place itself barely existed before the Germans came: a little railway station serving a scatter of local villages, no more than that. In 1941 a penal camp of Poles, mainly Christian but with Jews among them, began to work a nearby quarry. Then in May of 1942 there was an influx of Jewish workers, some from the penal camp, more rounded up in neighbouring towns, and rumours of land being cleared and fenced, a well being dug. A complex of buildings with some unusual installations rose swiftly, mysteriously, in the forest four kilometres from the little railway station, which was now connected to the new complex by a branch line.

Only four Nazi camps were dedicated exclusively to murder: Chelmno, Belzec, Sobibor and Treblinka. The extermination camp at Auschwitz-Birkenau, in time the largest of them all, was embedded within a cluster of pre-existing work and holding camps, as was the smaller Majdaneck. All of the death camps were established in Poland, with its many Jews and its fine railway system capable of delivering more and more. Chelmno was functioning, if less than efficiently, by December of 1941. The other three were in operation by July 1942.

The Treblinka camp was the last to be built, the first to be closed, and for much of its existence the most efficient. Like the earlier model at Sobibor it was contained within an oblong of land 600 by 400 metres bounded by a three-metre barbed wire fence. Within that boundary fence was another fence, also three metres high and of barbed wire, and punctuated by taller watchtowers, the whole being surmounted by floodlights: the features we now recognise as standard for the concentration camp, Nazi-style

Treblinka was Nazism in full flower. If the internal order of every concentration camp embodied the Nazi vision of society—the savagely differentiated racial hierarchy, the conscious, merciless pitting of isolated individuals one against the other—Treblinka was its fatal consummation: the mass production of unindividuated death. That resolution might not have been clearly envisioned in 1940, but it was the natural extension of a deranged idea that willed first a Germany, then a Europe, cleansed of every last one of its Jews. It was not a popular vision: it was limited to the most dedicated Nazis, and the formal extension from ideology to systematic annihilation was kept largely secret from homeland Germans by official silence, the silence imposed by threat and fearful rumour, and (not least) the numbed silence imposed by the systematic perversion of language.

Treblinka had its particular refinements. Its barbed wire was intricately interwoven with green pine branches, as were the major divisions inside the camp. What was done within these high green walls could be smelled and heard, but not seen. A piled-earth wall divided the enclosed oblong into the two separate zones of the Upper and the Lower camps. There was only one main passageway between the two sectors, again bounded by high barbed wire, again swathed in pine branches, with a bend in it to baffle sight. The passage was known to the camp's more permanent inmates as 'the Tube'.

The Lower Camp contained accommodation and kitchens for a thousand work-Jews, including among them perhaps fifty women, a hundred or so Ukrainian guards, and the forty SS assigned to the camp. The SS alternated in service, so there were usually only twenty in the camp at any one time. They preferred to use underlings to do the hands-on work.

All of the SS and most of the Jewish and Ukrainian camp personnel lived inside the Lower Camp, and it was there that the first work of reception, selection and processing of the incoming trainloads was done. The station platform gave directly onto the 'reception area'. Released from their trains, the deportees, nearly all of them Jews but with a few Gypsies and other nationalities mixed in, were divested of their clothing and possessions in the undressing barracks under the usual pretext of 'disinfection', and then ejected into the Tube to be driven naked along its length and flogged up the shallow stairs into the gas chambers. The doors were closed, the gas pumped in—and the work of the Lower Camp was finished.

The destruction of the corpses was the charge of the workers of the Upper Camp. Their task was to drag the tangled bodies from the chambers, to search body cavities for hidden wealth, to remove gold dental work, and then to obliterate the remains. During the first months of operation the corpses were buried in great pits inside the upper compound, but later, with bodies piling up and decomposition slow, both fresh and exhumed corpses were burnt on metal grids in troughs of fire and the ashes disposed of in ash pits.

When the work was efficiently done—and Treblinka's longest-serving Commandant Franz Stangl was famously efficient—up to seven thousand people could be dealt with in the course of a single day. Treblinka received its first transport (from the Warsaw ghetto) on 23 July, 1942, and its last in October of 1943. In its brief life of fourteen months the camp processed nine hundred thousand living bodies into smoke, grease and ashes.

As for survivors: a handful of work-Jews managed to escape by hiding among the bales of clothing they had sorted and packed for dispatch to Germany. Then in August of 1943 a desperate uprising and mass breakout by largely unarmed prisoner-workers cost the lives of hundreds of the rebels. Of those who escaped into the Polish forests no more than seventy evaded the manhunts and managed to stay alive until they were rescued by the Soviet army almost a year later. Meanwhile, the camp, its work done, had been closed. After the processing of a few last trainloads of victims the surviving work-Jews were set to demolishing the camp's remaining structures, and to ploughing the soiled earth, which they replanted with trees. They also built a farm house—using bricks from the old gas chambers—where a Ukrainian couple was installed and instructed to swear they had been living there, peacefully farming, for years. With all traces of Treblinka erased, the last of its Jews were shipped to Sobibor to be gassed.

Treblinka had ceased to exist—had been obliterated, made to vanish, disappeared—by the supreme and potent will of the Nazi state. In time that erasure was to be contested by a survivor of that heroic, doomed prisoner uprising. After a year in the forest, with the Russians come at last, Chaim Sztajer set off to search for any surviving kin. He already knew that his young wife, his child, his parents and his brothers had died in Treblinka because he had been 'selected for labour' from the same transport. But perhaps the Nazis had missed an aunt, or a cousin? He went first to his Polish homeplace, where it was as if the Jews had never been, then to Germany. There he found a niece. The rest were gone. Then he went to Israel, and later to Australia.

Chaim Sztajer knew Treblinka well. After two weeks of sorting clothing in the Lower Camp he had been transferred to the Upper Camp, so becoming one of the very few men to work in both the Lower and the Upper camps. Now in his mid-eighties, he is still a strong, quick-moving man, so it must have been his size and strength that sent him to the Upper Camp, and then helped him survive it.

He is also a man of skilled hands, and of prodigious memory. Once financially established in his new country and with his new family secure, he chose to spend several years of his life subverting his Nazi overlords' attempt to obliterate their shared history. He built destroyed Treblinka anew on a vast table in his St Kilda house. He did the work, he says, in a spirit of lamentation, but the defiance of his testament stands.

It is Chaim's model of Treblinka that provides the focal point of the Holocaust Museum's display. I have seen a number of two-dimensional plans of Treblinka, and tried to absorb them; examining them soberly, carefully matching the number in this square to that descriptive tag. It was a laborious business, and at the end the plan on the paper was transferred into my head and that was all that has happened. All that peering and matching had worked like a sedative upon the imagination: the image lay flat and flaccid, obstinately abstract, obstinately dead.

The effect of the model Treblinka is very different. One long glance can comprehend the whole organisation. It is possible to grasp the terrible simplicity of its informing concept; to feel the presence of minds that could so sleekly analyse the 'problem' of effecting mass human death at maximum speed with minimum fuss and the efficient utilisation of all possible by-products. The extermination camps are often called 'death factories'. The metaphor captures the reduction of human dreams, love, terror and despair to purely physical modules and the ruthlessly mechanical sequencing of those modules, but it obscures their terrifying simplicity. There was nothing technically complicated, nothing 'industrial', about Treblinka. There was almost no machinery beyond a mechanical ditch-digger. Why should there be, when there was an inexhaustible human labour supply that cost precisely nothing? Human hands, a few simple tools—shovels, poles with iron hooks, makeshift stretchers—and the work was done. If the death camps were factories, they were very primitive ones.

What the model shows most clearly is how easy mass murder is when emptied of human scruple and emotion. Except for the jocular attempts to deceive the more gullible among its victims (the arch above the station entrance read 'Rehabilitation and Work-Camp for Jews'), Treblinka might as well have been an abattoir.

Chaim Sztajer's model reveals only externals. It cannot show us the horror behind wood and metal: what happened inside the trains, what happened inside the buildings. Deportees were brought to the camp in sealed trains, western Jews typically in 'normal' if overcrowded carriages, easterners crammed into cattle trucks with the doors nailed shut and every residual aperture stuffed with barbed wire. They were given no food or water for the duration of the passage, there were no sanitary provisions, and these trains, with nil priority on the track, travelled slowly. The journey from Warsaw, normally a two-hour trip, could take up to twelve hours when the cargo was Jews and the destination Treblinka. We do not see what happened inside the trains. We do not see the frantic haste of the team of work-Jews scouring those incoming cars of the filth of their human cargo to make way for the next set. (The camp siding could take only twenty cars at a time: most trains pulled sixty.) The model shows us a token litter of clothing and possessions in the sorting yard. We do not see the mountains of clothing and boots, blankets and foodstuffs which rose up with the arrival of the richest trains. We do not see the desperate intricacy of the lives lived inside the oblong wooden boxes labelled 'Living Quarters for Work-Jews', or the very different lives lived within the boxes named 'For Ukrainian Guards' and 'SS'. We do not see inside the undressing barracks—the bewilderment, the humiliation of nakedness, the mounting dread. We do not see the numb waiting inside the gas chambers, or the clambering, choking, panic. We do not hear the screams.

The model is nonetheless a stunningly effective visual representation; for its portrait of the Nazi mind, but also for another more elusive reason. Chaim Sztajer was and remains a formidable craftsman. The model is, as he proudly says, 'exact', in its proportions, in the distribution of its shapes. However, it is not the exactitude that mesmerises. What makes it so powerfully disturbing?

The secret lies, I think, precisely in its inexactitudes. Sztajer had been a professional carpenter. The wooden structures in the compounds are neatly built and as neatly painted (dark green). He was not, however, a professional model-maker. His resources through the years of construction remained local and domestic, so there is a dis-locating tincture of childhood charm in his creation. Many of the objects he brought together to effect his testament to memory—the little train, sleek in its maroon and cream enamel, the curving metal tracks, the sturdy navy-blue ditch-digger in the Upper Camp, Commandant Stangl's shining white horse—come directly from the toyshop. We feel some of that familiar magic again as we marvel at the huts, at the tiny figures, at all the lovely, miniaturised detail. Then we see the menace in the train's metallic sleekness, and that the ditch-digger clutches a rag of flesh in its dark blue claw.

The fabrication of those high walls unleashes another complicated response. Sztajer used ordinary barbed wire—real-size barbed wire—to make the barbed wire pen within a barbed wire pen that was Treblinka. This raises a jolting issue of scale. Measured against the little 'fighting men' figures that are now distributed along the walkways between the watchtowers, the barbed wire is much too large, much too coarse. But at the same moment we see that—I think *because* we see that—we see how brutal those iron knots are: how sharp the spines, how cruelly they would grip and tear human flesh. We are jerked into sudden close-up; to *see* the wire we do not see when it rims familiar paddocks and threatens only animals.

Necessity forced invention. In Treblinka the barbed wire had been swathed with fresh pine branches. How to replicate that? Sztajer solved the problem, ingeniously, ingenuously, by using the shining green plastic wadding butchers and fruiterers use to set off their wares. The green looks painfully artificial under the electric light. At first it also seems incongruous: associations with the daily and the domestic jangle in the head. But the walls of the model are thick, and green, and stifling, and another survivor searching for words to describe the walls of the 'green trap' of Treblinka described them as 'green walls covered with a pine needle pelt', so perhaps the shopkeepers' plastic is not far off the mark after all.

It is the human figures that rivet attention. All the permanent inhabitants—the SS men, the Ukrainian guards, the work-Jews—are solid. Made of lead or plastic, painstakingly painted (again that whiff of childhood), they are dressed in tiny reproductions of their uniforms and distinguishing caps, black for the Ukrainians, grey-green for the SS ('Exact!'). Even the naked bodies of two would-be escapees hanging upside-down on the gibbet look solid, naked, real.

By contrast the transients, those who are to die in the gas, look—transient. The figures spilling from the train and proceeding along the path to the undressing barracks are immaculately cut from stiff paper, and as immaculately coloured in: men and women, a rabbi, grey-beards, children holding hands, a tall thin man with a case. It must be because of the crayoned paper that they look so fragile, so touchingly neat, even cheerful, in their brightly-coloured clothing, marching along the narrow path. They conjure children marching gaily into school.

We see them again as they emerge from the undressing barracks into the Tube—or half-see them. They are difficult to see in the dim light between the funnelling green walls, but it is clear that now they are naked. And now they are solid: small pale solid naked dolls. There are some artificial flowers along the path, made out of something moulded, possibly ceramic, like the flowers you see on Greek and Italian graves. These cemetery flowers stand for the flowerbeds the Germans ordered planted along the Tube. The Germans also often stationed three musicians against the curving wall to play, some say chamber music, some say waltzes, but Sztajer decided against including them. Credulity has its limits.

As for the Upper Camp—this has been a contested area between maker and museum. Sztajer had originally used small pink plastic dolls to represent the corpses dragged from the gas chambers. He had spitted one tiny one on the end of a pitchfork held by one of the guards. The museum custodians decided to remove them: the dolls, the spitted baby, might make visiting schoolboys laugh. Perhaps they would have laughed. But babies were speared on pitchforks in Treblinka.

The dolls have been replaced by greyish-white plaster-of-Paris figures, and it is true one does not want to laugh at them. But they do not look like human corpses. Their transformation is too complete. They look like figures made out of ash. They are also large, much larger than the little figures who tug them or heave them or lug them on stretchers. And again, incongruity serves a purpose. Their unwieldiness remind us how very large and recalcitrant these corpses must have seemed to the men who sweated to reduce them to weightless air and ashes.

Chaim has placed Commandant Stangl in the reception area of the Lower Camp, watching the arrival of a trainload of victims, in his smart white jacket, on his smart white horse, as he so often used to watch. Beside him stands Kurt Franz, 'the Doll', Stangl's immediate subordinate and the most handsome, happy and murderous of all the SS guards. (Kurt Franz, sentenced to life imprisonment at his trial in 1965, was granted his freedom in Germany late last year. Chaim Sztajer trembled uncontrollably when he told me that Kurt Franz was once again free in their shared world.) Beside Franz is his big Alsatian Bari, trained to savage the genitals of the naked creatures running the length of the Tube.

Once there were more figures inside the model. The museum curators took them out, Sztajer says bitterly, he doesn't know why—three Germans, one Jewish man, and 'most' of the Ukrainians. I suppose they took them out because they made the camp look cluttered. But the reality must have been cluttered too, with so many Ukrainians about, and every one of them looking for someone to hit.

Some of the SS figures have guns. The guns are painted black. Others, especially the Ukrainians, hold whips. Again attention is snagged by the incongruity of scale. The whips are too large, they trail well beyond the boots of the men holding them. Treblinka whips were plaited from narrow strips of leather, sometimes with a wire core. These whips have been plaited from narrow strips of leather too, so of course they are too large. Later I discover that some of the real whips were very long; that one was so long it used to tangle around the feet of the guard who wielded it. One survivor remembers his first sight of the platform at Treblinka was of men wearing blue armbands, one of them holding a whip 'not like any whip I'd ever seen, but like something for big animals'. The whips must have looked very large to the prisoners. Perhaps they are not too large after all.

Other changes were made to the model after Sztajer handed it over to the museum. He is reconciled to none of them. The little soldiers that now line the walkways between the watchtowers, bayonet-lunging at empty air, shooting at the sky, don't look like Germans. They look like American soldiers from a child's army set.

Originally he had distributed them between the Upper and the Lower camps. 'In reality'—an odd notion, inside surreal Treblinka—there had been no soldiers in the camp, which is why the curators took them away. But there was always the sound of shooting, and the likelihood of being shot. Some of the SS made a hobby of shooting men for sport. For prisoners Treblinka was a war zone. The aggressive little soldiers set thickly about might have been intended to tell us that.

Incongruities of material, incongruities of scale—discordant memories. What seems to come out of this is that models are most effective in their imperfections, when incongruities act like a constantly jabbing finger: *Attend now! So it was not like this? Why not? How, then, was it?* They do not allow the eye to skim, the attention to wander. We have to think, and to keep thinking; to imagine, and to keep imagining. The jarring images goad imagination, activate unwilling knowledge, force flinching memory, providing the shock essential for deep communication, whether of information or of feeling. They force one not to mere 'watching', but to the emotional comprehension of experiences not our own.

All miniaturisations are initially disarming because of our association of miniaturisation with childhood; a child's delight in having its own marvellous, intricate, docile little world to play with, to possess in its miniaturised perfection. We respond to that innocence. (We are less attentive to the implied megalomania.) There was another committed model-maker at Treblinka whose masterpiece we can no longer see because he ordered it destroyed: the one person who customarily viewed Treblinka, as we do the model, comprehensively, from an elevation.

Guards and prisoners remember Franz Stangl standing alone on the sandy rise that divided the two sections of the camp, surveying his domain, drawing pleasure from what he saw, and tirelessly devising improvements and embellishments. It was Stangl who decided that the business would run more smoothly if work-Jews were not killed casually but kept alive long enough to become skilled in their particular tasks; who decided that the tiny space where hair was shorn from the heads of naked women and children in the Tube should be screened to reduce panic. He even considered placing buckets for evacuation along the length of the Tube, but decided against it: after all, it would slow things down, and there were plenty of hands to clean up afterwards.

If his main concern was to keep the killing operation fluent, he also relished administrative detail. In preparation for a major inspection by Adolph Eichmann he devised ever-finer categories for the labelling of the storage trunks of the possessions of slaughtered Jews, and was duly praised for it. Eichmann appreciated detail, too.

But his private pleasure, indeed his obsession, was the beautification of the Lower Camp. In the spring of 1943, with most of Europe's Jews already dead and the transports slowing, he had both the time and the labour to implement some of his choicer refinements. What he did first was what any child model-maker would do: he cleaned up his quadrangle of ground, and then proceeded to add beguiling details to facilitate make believe.

There had always been one corner of Treblinka that was pure make believe. Aged or infirm prisoners too physically or mentally unstable for their legs to carry them through 'normal' processing were walked directly from the train to a small structure with a red cross painted on the front. It was called 'the infirmary', or, less formally, the 'Lazarette'. Once through the doorway the prisoners would see that this was not a hospital but a theatrical set, containing no more than a weather-shelter for the guard, a table and bench set to one side, and a long, low earthen wall. 'Helped' to undress, they were then sat on the wall and shot in the neck, their bodies falling into the fire-pit on the other side. The infirmary was also the killing site for debilitated or refractory prisoners from the Lower Camp. Punishment in the Upper Camp was by the more declamatory public forms, by shooting, or hanging.

I have written elsewhere on the elaborate theatre developed by the SS at Auschwitz-Birkenau: a theatre designed not only to lull their victims into compliance but to gratify the star performers themselves. At Treblinka the devices to deceive were, initially, more perfunctory. Incomers from the west were usually greeted gently, and some effort made to reassure them—separate disrobing areas for men and women, soap distributed—until they were ejected into the Tube and running naked under the whips. Trains from the east carrying people who had learnt what to expect were met by some of those Ukrainian 'helpers' wielding their whips and bludgeons. Force, always immanent, was made manifest for the reception of cargo from the cattle trucks from the east.

With a lull in the killing and time and labour on his hands, Stangl was able to indulge himself. The whole Lower Camp—separated from the gas chambers and the corpse-burning racks of the Upper Camp only by that pine-wreathed wire fence—was beautified. A street was constructed: '800 metres, all bordered with flowers', with garden beds and walks, and wooden benches dotting the landscape 'like a luxury spa'. Elaborate furbelows were added to the railway station: a fake clock, its hands pointing eternally to six o'clock, fake ticket windows, fake signs promising 'Trains to Bialystok', 'to Wolkowisk', 'to Warsaw'; signs pointing to 'The Baths'. On the back wall a fake door was painted and labelled 'Stationmaster': a splendid piece of *trompe l'oeil*. Kurt Franz is given credit for the establishment of a Zoo Corner, which held 'two foxes, a few squirrels and pigeons, and a variety of other small animals', along with a stable, a pigsty and a small chicken yard. The work on the zoo was done by an eighteen-year-old prisoner who was also responsible for its paths of sifted yellow sand edged by gardens and low birch fences. A little later the improvement to camp paths was extended, the railway station being done out in black cinders and all the paths of the Lower Camp in shining yellow sand edged with multicoloured stone. And at every corner there was a hand-carved wooden sign: an SS symbol indicated the SS quarters, a crooked wooden Jew pointed with one long carved finger 'To The Ghetto'. The whole was crowned, as Stangl happily remembered for Gitta Sereny three decades later, by a guardhouse 'in Tyrolean style...I tell you, I had the best carpenters in the world—everyone envied me. It was all done in wood—stylistically perfect'—although, as he ruefully acknowledged, 'the whole place stank to high heaven from kilometres away'.

At Buchenwald, deep inside German territory, the SS had their prisoners create a luxurious hunting lodge in old Germanic style, and maintained a deer park and a zoo with 'monkeys, bears and a rhinoceros, a falconry and cages containing wild cats'—décor for the dreams of an ersatz Germanic aristocracy. These were lusher fantasies than could be sustained in a decrepit corner of Poland. The 'improvements' at Treblinka expose Stangl's more bourgeois vision, as—ignoring the stench, ignoring the reality—he strove to render the environment of the Treblinka SS charming, cosy, *gemütlich*.

Stangl played with Treblinka as if it were his personal toyshop. Responsible for every detail, he cared about every detail. Standing on the rise between the two sections, he gloated over the world he had made. One of the handful of escapees from Sobibor to survive the war remembers Stangl coming to watch him at work (he was a talented goldsmith) before his transfer to Treblinka. Sam Szmajzner remembers Stangl not for his cruelty—indeed, he never saw him inflict pain on anybody—but for the pleasure he took in his work. Szmajzner remembered: 'He had this perpetual smile on his face.' Then, in answer to a question from the interviewer: 'No, I don't think it was a nervous smile. It was just that he was happy.'

Chaim Sztajer's model of Treblinka is memory actualised. Is it also a vengeance taken? Its maker says not: that it is a memorial to those who died, and only that: a memorial to them, and to his grief. His daughter, born to the wife he married in Israel and growing up in Australia, remembers him weeping as he worked. But in the lonely hours spent shaping the wood and painting it, cutting and colouring the paper figures, haunting toyshops to find the dolls he would transform into people; in the patience of the reconstruction and the intensity fuelling the patience, in the difficulties overcome, the solutions arrived at—surely these actions must have assuaged the bitterness of his past helplessness? His SS overlords denied his human worth, as they denied the reality of Treblinka. Through his model he has insisted on both.

Now his private re-creation has been recognised by the curators as the work of art it is. It must therefore be properly preserved and reverently presented. The floodlights he installed in his passion for exactitude have therefore been removed, and the model sealed behind glass. These changes cause its maker anguish. Despite the clarity of his memory for things, Sztajer's memory for people seems to have been frightened into hiding for much of his time in the camp. Of all the SS men he remembers only two, one of them the vicious Kurt Franz, the other a 'very kind man' who worked in the Upper Camp. His memory comes to life again for the Polish Jews and Christians met in the forest after his escape, and for the ex-Treblinka prisoners he later found miraculously alive in Israel. But not for his time inside Treblinka. Not for his time among the dead.

He rages, as artists will, at the changes that the curators made and at the abduction and sealing-away of his creation. But I think his grief is more than that. Now he can no longer touch his past; no longer commune by way of clipped paper, wood and wire, by small additions and adjustments, with his own younger self; with the beloved people and the hopes obliterated in Treblinka. Now Chaim Sztajer weeps because his past has been taken away from him and sealed behind glass.

2000

III SECRET LIVES

SECRET MEETINGS, SECRET LIVES

Over the last years there has come to be a *de facto* division of labour regarding biographies. Historians take on the public figures—explorers, generals, politicians, the more respectable tycoons—while people I would loosely call literary critics tackle the painters and poets, the novelists and dramatists. Sporting heroes and criminals tend to fall to journalists and (increasingly) the Culture Studies people.

On the face of it, historians ought to have the best of the bargain: after all, they get the movers and shakers, while what most writers do, save for the few with a taste for flaming and burning out, is sit quietly in their rooms and write. It has not turned out like that. Public figures are primarily interesting for what they publicly do. While we sniff the air to catch the least whiff of corruption, while we rake over the family ashes to discover the ember glowing with the itch for power, what most of us most want to know is how they got power, how they used it, how they lost it, and what they achieved or failed to achieve by it. That prescribes Antecedents, Rise, Achievements, Influence, with a side-trip into Family Life and a bob to the ladies. With psycho-biographers the ratio reverses, with the side-trip becoming the main journey, but the aim remains constant: to give a behind-the-scenes explanation of what we see up there on the big screen; the public woman or the public man in action. There is still the sense with such a person that once the flood of memoirs and gossip is over, a single, solidly researched biography will see the end of them; that with the last memorandum read, the last resonance in the last entry in the funeral book recorded, they will be definitively, finally 'done'.

Political biographies are not a growth industry. By contrast, over the last couple of decades the literary biography has not only been cantering away from its political brother, but routinely outselling all other forms of narrative history. Everyone seems to be reading them, and (given writers' desire to eat) everyone seems to be writing them. The reasons for this vast public appetite are mysterious. It is not as if writers have much influence nowadays. We do not look to them for moral exhortation, or for exaltation, either. Is it scandal we are after? Do we still believe that art is a flower of the swamp, that the biography of the artist might yield the sweaty revelations we know we will never get from autobiographies, that most fictive of literary forms? Janet Malcolm thinks so, and Janet Malcolm, intrepid biographer, is in a position to know. Precisely a century ago Henry James predicted what would happen when literary snooping came to be accorded respectability:

> Then at last the game will be fair and the two forces face to face; it will be 'pull, devil, pull, tailor', and the hardest pull will doubtless provide the happiest result. Then the cunning of the inquirer, envenomed with resistance, will exceed in subtlety and ferocity anything we today conceive, and the pale forewarned victim, with every track covered, every paper burnt and every letter unanswered, will, in the tower of art, the invulnerable granite, stand, without a sally, the siege of all the years.

James wrote these magnificently paced phrases to preface his gentlemanly reflections on the scandalous George Sands. Malcolm, with terrifying aplomb, appropriates them as epigraph for her book on Sylvia Plath and Ted Hughes. Blanch, victim. Let the cash registers ring.

It is true that times have changed and that even the most scholarly biographers practise ruthlessness these days. But I am still not persuaded that it is scandal we are after, although we will take it if it is on offer. We are no longer bamboozled by the likes of Byron, Kerouac or the deplorable Nin; we know that by and large writers do not live lurid lives and then dash home to scribble down the highlights for our delectation. We know that writers' daily lives are dull. So why the hunger?

Consider the 'Demidenko affair' when a young woman named Helen Darville took on the identity of Helen Demidenko, a fictional character of her own making, in which persona she wrote a novel called *The Hand That Signed the Paper*. The affair was in every one of its several mutations painfully instructive: on the distinction between history and fiction, on when appropriation becomes plagiarism, and so on. But it was the author's deception regarding her own identity that so outraged all the combatants, including those who had admired the Demidenko novel most, as to end discussion. We felt ourselves to have been betrayed. We felt the earth slip.

Coolly considered, this was an odd response. After all, the woman's awards were for fiction, so what did it matter whether she had learnt Ukrainian horrors at her grandfather's knee or from some insufficiently acknowledged book? I grant that this was a special case: that the daughter-of-Ukrainian-suffering claim was a political weapon, and a vigorously used weapon at that, so that anger was added to outrage, but what interests me is the more subterranean response. Is it that we feel that authenticity in fiction depends on direct or directly communicated experience, an apostolic succession of veracity? Surely not: we do not insist that Nabokov be a paedophile, or Kafka a beetle. We may think we have learnt something important about Aharon Appelfeld's novels when we learn that Appelfeld and his family had been scooped up by the Nazis from a town in Bukhovina, that his mother was shot, and he and his father dispatched to a concentration camp; that he, aged eight, escaped from the train to live for three years in the forests of the Ukraine until the Russians came; that he fetched up in Israel and wrote his novels there; that he chose to write in Hebrew—but what is it that we have learnt? I discovered those facts well after I had discovered and been astounded by the novels.

Why are we so curious about the 'who' who writes when that 'who' is writing fiction? We are not curious about historians, or political scientists. We may want to know something about their class background or career path to make some limp adjustment for 'bias,' but we have not the least interest in their sensibility. It is literary artists we want to know better. Post-modernists might tell us that the author is immaterial, that all we need, want or can have is the text; we do not believe them. When Philip Roth says: 'As for my autobiography, I can't begin to tell you how dull it would be. [It] would consist almost entirely of chapters about me sitting alone in a room looking at a typewriter,' we know he is telling the truth. But we continue insatiable. We want to know everything he does down to the minutiae of his days: if spent at a desk, what kind of desk, on what kind of chair, chewing what kind of pen, tapping at what keyboard, for how long at a time? When does he eat? When does he sleep? Do we care whom he sleeps with? Yes we do. But we care more about knowing how long he sleeps, in what kind of bed, whether he dreams and, if he dreams, what the dreams are about.

What moves us is a kind of love. It is also, as love can be, an obsession, a kind of sickness. Recognising its reality, however little they may understand it, writers defend themselves, just as James predicted. They issue prohibitions. They plan, and sometimes effect, whole holocausts of documents. They die, an extreme strategy and, the laws of libel being what they are, an ineffectual one; they play dead, like J. D. Salinger, which is only marginally less so. They play dull, like Anthony Trollope. Some play dragon, like Nabokov in his high Genevan citadel, lounging on his heaps of gold, emitting great whorls of obscuring fumes, daring us poor daunted doting mortals to approach. But we, mad with love, will not leave off: circling, blinking, peering tearily through the smoke, we watch for any sign, even of fury. Why? What are we yearning for?

We do not feel the same passion for everybody who happens to make marks on paper which then sell well. Consider the case of Mrs Frances Milton Trollope. When failing family fortunes sent her, aged fifty three, with her clutch of dependent children to the United States of America, she returned to England with a manuscript called *Domestic Manners of the Americans*, which was so lively that many Americans still have not forgiven her. So began a writing career that ended only with her breath twenty-seven years later, leaving her children grown and rosy and forty-one books published. Surely a salutary life, well worth retrieving? But no one, even in these days of reassembling the shattered fragments of women left devastated in the wake of some Great White Male, will bother to reassemble Mrs Trollope. She will never have a biography. (*Stop Press*. March 1997. Never make public predictions. Ms Trollope has just been awarded two. She also turns out to be a wit. When accused of the too-direct translation of acquaintances into fiction, she tartly responded: 'I always pulp my acquaintances before serving them up. You would never recognise a pig in a sausage.')

Meanwhile her son Anthony, features muffled by tufting hair and spectacles, his correspondence studiously commonplace, his life an open ledger, has had three 'admirably detailed' biographies since 1988, all splendidly fat ('merely opening any of them is sufficient to endanger the spine'), and with another to come. And, presumably, more, either in press or in mind. Trollope, knowing he was going to be under siege post-mortem, had attempted the pre-emptive strike of writing an autobiography of his own to be published posthumously: the final, deliberate blurring of tracks. He ends his self-accounting on a majestically flat note:

> It will not, I trust, be supposed by any reader that I have intended...to give a record of my inner life...If the rustle of a woman's petticoats has ever stirred my blood; if a cup of wine has been a joy to me; if I have thought tobacco at midnight in pleasant company to be one of the elements of an earthly Paradise; if now and again I have somewhat recklessly fluttered a five pound note over a card table:—of what matter is that to any reader?

This is truly splendid technique: after that string of flaccid banalities, what matter indeed? We are stopped, yelping, in our tracks. Nonetheless...remember those three biographies in less than a decade, and more coming.

Why? Our infatuated pursuit of studiously dull Trollope gives us the clue. What we are yearning for is more fuel for our love. We burn to get our hands not on the public and published, not even on the personal and private, but on the Writer's Inner Life—even when (as with Trollope) that inner life 'appeared either indistinguishable from his public image, irrecoverable because of the lack of documents, or simply non-existent,' as a reviewer put it. But we are not satisfied. We suspect, indeed we insist, that there must be another Life somewhere further in. We are certain that every artist, including Trollope, has one: that somewhere behind those well-polished light-reflecting windows, those pruned lawns and hedges, a prince is hiding. We know he is a prince because he has a kingdom: a small, solid, delightfully coherent place that we can visit as often as we want: a place where we know, or will very soon know, everything that is going on. There is no other place in the world like it, and Trollope holds the key. We talk of 'Dickens's London' or of 'Jane Austen's England', and that is precisely what we mean: the little worlds they have made for us to live in. Trollopesville is not diaphanous. It is not in the least fantastical. Its particular magic is to be simpler, smaller and very much cosier than the actual world could ever be. We like it there.

We also feel at home with Trollope's people. I have written just enough fiction to discover the paranoia of friends at once terrified that you will 'use' them, and affronted by the possibility that you will not. What I would like to say to them (and don't, because it would be useless) is that they are much too complex, multiple and mysterious to be of any use to me; that even if I filch a gesture, a tilt of chin, a twirl of conscience to adorn some invented person, no person on the page is or could be them because I do not know them sufficiently well to take such liberties. Someone glimpsed or marginally known is easy grist to the fiction writer's mill. Intimates are not. Familiarity only breeds darker opacities, dim oceans beyond the fringing reef of the known.

(Which reminds me: for some of us passionate readers there is another and mildly pathetic motive: the wistful desire to emulate. We hunger for every detail in the hope the magicians might let the secret slip, that they will tell us how they create those whole entrancing worlds we find at the end of their beanstalks of words. The hope is vain. Salman Rushdie, asked how he had come to write *Midnight's Children*—absurd, irresistible question—answered that he had been looking at a map of India one day and noticed that it looked like a big nose, with Sri Lanka the drip at the end. So he wrote a book about a boy with a big, dripping nose. An honest answer, we have to assume, but an answer which is no help at all.)

I think our envy at the variety and the coherence of the fiction writer's inventive power is the core reason why we abandon decency and pry where we should not; why we encourage our agents to rifle private papers, abscond with letters and lure reluctant informants into ersatz confessionals the better to betray them. Who cares about world-shakers? It is the world-makers we want, and we are desperate to know how they do it.

Phillip Roth again, but this time as reader: 'I read fiction to be freed from my own suffocatingly narrow perspective on life and to be lured into imaginative sympathy with a fully developed narrative point of view not my own.' A 'fully developed narrative point of view': another world indeed, but unlike our actual worlds a coherent and complete one: a world where the weather is always as it ought to be (those Chekhovian springs, those Nabokovian winters) and will never disappoint us. And where we will always find a friend ready for our company. These world-makers are reliable. They are never offended when we break off our talk; when we pick them up again there they are, tranquilly waiting to resume. With them, and only with them, we can continue the conversation we have with ourselves in our heads—the conversation we thought we could have only with ourselves.

We cannot easily bear to lose that intimacy when we see that the words stop halfway down the next page, that the page after that is blank, that the stiff back cover is poised to close on our joys like the lid of a coffin. The sense of being cast out of a magic kingdom is perhaps strongest when we are dealing with those consummate stylists (Shakespeare? Flaubert? Nabokov?) theoretically most absent from the text. It is marginally more painful with those few, like Flaubert and Chekhov, who write letters almost as luminous as their fictional writings, or like Plath, whose 'private' journals incandesce. But only marginally: we know that the most intense communication comes through their most perfect, most distilled art. This is a companionship of a kind and quality unavailable in the 'real' world. It is also why I think the book will survive all challenges. There it is, ready for the hand, waiting between its silent covers. And this is why we consume literary biographies like buns hot from the oven.

There may be a further reason. The most successful literary biographies have been very big books indeed. Could it be that in these lonely and unstable times we want the reassurance of big books, books with a solid story, a steady temporal progression, a pleasantly various cast of well-marked characters—all the kinds of things nineteenth-century novelists (and historians) used to provide, and late-twentieth-century novelists (and historians) do not? My private suspicion is that these fat-to-gross biographies fill something of the void left by the demise of the Late Victorian novel, heavy on the knee, thick under the thumb, where we could have a secure sense of knowing What Was Going On and wait for the next leisurely, spacious, populous episode with confidence. Consider how our lives were changed for the duration of the televised series 'Pride and Prejudice', how grateful we were for our regular Sunday invitation into that melodious, richly peopled tale. And then Darcy and Elizabeth drove off into their well-conducted future, and everyone else went home. And we were left outside.

1997

THE CRACK IN THE TEACUP: READING HILARY MANTEL

About a decade ago I picked up a book because I liked the cover: a bleak street, stark buildings, empty sky, a robed man, his back turned, in the distance; in the foreground a woman in a burqa with her head turned to the left, looking at something we can't see. When the blurb promised me 'a Middle Eastern *Turn of the Screw*, with an insidious power to grip', I bought it. It gripped. In fact, it scared the living bejasus out of me. That was my introduction to Hilary Mantel's writings. Since then, I have read nearly everything she has published.

Eight Months on Ghazzah Street (1988) is about a sensible young British couple who, after years of humanitarian work in Africa, decide to go to Saudi Arabia to repair their fortunes. The husband will work on a seductively extravagant building project; the wife will read, write and relax in their pleasant, if mildly claustrophobic, apartment. Then small things begin to go wrong…

I read it, reread it, read it in slow motion, read parts of it backwards, and I still could not see how Mantel had done it. Nothing much happens, or nothing you see, but dread comes oozing down an empty stairwell, under a sealed door, into a quiet apartment, and there is nothing you can do to resist it even on the fourth reading. Then I read the other novels. One robust reviewer declared a couple of the more gothic ones, *Every Day is Mother's Day* (1985) and *Vacant Possession* (1986), were comedies, and I do remember laughing. At first. Before my flesh began to creep. Others, such as *Fludd* (1989) and *The Giant, O'Brien* (1998), are overtly fables, but an insidious cruelty is their engine. Finally I arrived at the novel that Mantel had begun first, *A Place of Greater Safety* (1992). Set in the French Revolution, it has characters named 'Maximilien Robespierre' and 'Camille Demouslins', so I decided not to read it. As an historian, I am snooty about historical novels. Besides, I knew the plot. Now, after reading Mantel's recent memoir, *Giving up the Ghost*, I will read it.

I also read Mantel's critical essays as they appeared in the *London Review of Books* and the *New York Review of Books*. They kept getting better and better, in their clarity and in a rarer quality that I can only describe as intrepid intelligence. One of the most recent, on V. S. Naipaul, deepened my understanding and so my appreciation of his writings, which is what literary reviews are meant to do. Mantel values Naipaul's stylistic plainness because she practises it herself. She also knows about the costs and benefits of dislocation from the familiar. And they both know something darker: that injury is forever; that the people we damage will remain damaged, and forever dangerous.

Consider also this: 'Naipaul has a genius for noticing, a genius for freezing the instant when meaning is born from the accidents of the everyday.' Mantel shares that genius, though she takes a most ungenial view of accidents. In Mantel's world your 'accident' is waiting just for you. Sir Thomas Browne might warn: 'When all looks fair about, and thou seest not a cloud so big as a hand to threaten thee, forget not the wheel of things', but Browne's is altogether too cosy a vision for Mantel. All is never 'fair about'. There are always stirrings: intimations of danger made more unnerving by their mask of ordinariness. And there is no regulating wheel: only the sickening lurch from the everyday straight into horror. If you doubt me, read *A Change of Climate* (1994).

Late in 2001 I met a rather reticent woman called Hilary Mantel at the Adelaide Writers' Festival. I wasn't fooled. I knew I hadn't 'met the writer'. I knew that 'Hilary Mantel' only happened at her desk. This woman named Mantel and I fell into correspondence because she liked a short piece I had written for the *London Review of Books* on life, and intimations of death, after a liver transplant. Now that I have met her on the pages of *Giving up the Ghost*, I know why she liked it: because I had been respectful of a young woman whose girlish body had been swamped in flesh through the drugs she had to swallow to stay alive.

The same thing had happened—she says is still happening—to Mantel. The latter part of the memoir is largely to do with physical illness and its protean consequences. When she was seventeen, escaped at last to London from the constrictions of an unhappy home, embarked on a law degree and having met the man who would be her life companion, (in fact she married him twice) Mantel began to suffer disabling pains: pains that seemed to have the eerie power to migrate around her body. Endometriosis is a condition in which cells disperse from the lining of the womb to other parts of the body: to bowel, pelvis, heart, chest wall, head—everywhere. Being what they are, the migratory cells bleed; scar tissue forms; organs malfunction; pain happens. It is not a common condition, but neither is it rare. A half-way competent doctor should recognise it. A sequence of incompetent doctors diagnosed Mantel's problem as a severe case of female over-ambition, and dosed her with increasingly powerful psychiatric drugs, which very nearly made her mad. Ten destructive years later Mantel identified her condition from the books available in the public library of a dusty African town. By then it was too late: when she was twenty-seven, her womb and various other parts of her inner person had to be removed, and this in a woman with a visceral commitment to the continuity of families. (Reading this part of the memoir, I remembered that Mantel's work is haunted by the small unquiet ghosts of babies dead, or unborn, or lost, or stolen, or somehow mislaid: that ungrounded guilt is Mantel's familiar.) The disease, despite the surgery, reasserted itself, so after another bitter period of misdiagnosis Mantel began the hormone taking that buried her slight person in surplus flesh, and continues to impose its whimsical changes on her mind and body today.

This might seem to provide more than enough matter for a memoir, especially as these days most memoirs seem to focus on suffering: a well-creamed face stares dolefully from a page crowned by a title like 'I Survived', evoking a silent snarl: 'Survived what? Eyelid surgery?' Rather too many pivot on the notion of 'resilience': the human as high-quality tennis ball bouncing back into shape however hard you whack it. Nearly all are consolatory in both matter and tone. They assure us that suffering ennobles; that sweet resignation will be our crown at the end of weary years. I prefer the view embodied in the blues: loss hurts like a leg falling off, but you might make a good song out of it. Mantel believes that suffering is bad for you: that it makes you angry, and vengeful; that injury, whether wittingly or unwittingly inflicted, is an enduring outrage. She also believes that damage is irreparable, which, given that we have only one life, is seriously bad news.

The discussion of illness, scorching as it is, remains secondary in this remarkable book. Its bulk is taken up by Mantel's first fifteen years, with the emphasis on the first seven. Mantel's childhood is a puzzle to which she has found no solution. ('The story of my own childhood is a complicated sentence that I am always trying to finish, to finish and put behind me.') Born in 1952 in the grim town of Hadfield-near-Manchester, the first child of her parents, she spent her first years at the warm core of an Irish Catholic family of women—grandmother, aunts, great aunts, female cousins—with a grandfather as kindly patriarch. (Initially, her mother seems peripheral and her father more so; both increase in importance with time.)

Memoirists take a jealous interest in how other memoirists overcome the technical challenges they have struggled with themselves. (I have written a memoir.) Mantel's progress is marked by a glorious clatter of broken rules. She begins at the end, plunging into an account of a voluntary yet somehow coerced selling of a beloved house. The mood is fraught. On page one, she 'sees' a ghost on the stairs, then reassures us with a brisk account of what migraines can do to perception. She de-assures us two pages later when she tells us that she is so fond of this particular ghost (oppressive stepfather) that she 'can hardly bear to sell the cottage and leave him behind on the stairs'. She unnerves us by describing the 'migrainous sleep' that 'steals up' on her as an ogre who 'plants on my forehead a clammy ogre's kiss' and sucks her into oblivion. Then she remarks that she always sleeps well in this house. And there we are, dry-mouthed, already deep into Mantel territory.

She has no patience with orderly chronicling, and tosses it aside. In her twenties, Mantel spent some years in Botswana, where *A Change of Climate* is set, and a couple more in the Jeddah of *Eight Months on Ghazzah Street*, but she mentions Botswana only briefly and Jeddah not at all. Her concern is her inner history and tracking down the experiences that made it. After that ghost-haunted beginning, the narrative flicks from present to childhood to maturity to girlhood to deep family past and back again with a film-maker's élan. She is confident in her readers' ability to hold the narrative line and we do. Throughout the prose is utterly controlled, except for a brief moment early in the book—on page four, to be exact—when Mantel performs a small anxious jig about the tone she ought to adopt in writing a memoir. (I think this jig works psychologically as a war dance, a thought to which I will return.) Her anxiety is real, but we do not share it: after three pages, we are ready to follow her anywhere. Why? Because of the sheer power of the writing, which on the surface is clear, even matter-of-fact, but which has already seduced us into a previously unimagined world. Thereafter—braced for sinister experiences, seduced by a wry intelligence, nervously intuiting the rapids ahead—we commit ourselves to the current of the prose.

There are some quieter waters along the way. Mantel offers a beautifully dense description of lower-middle-class English provincial life in the 1950s and early 1960s, so providing the reliable pleasure of contemplating the recent past: younger readers can marvel at how their elders contrived to survive the squalor and deprivations of life 'back then' ('Your lavatory was at the end of the *garden*?'); the old can rub elderly backs against the pleasurable prickles of nostalgia. I had forgotten details of my own household until I met them again, immaculately described and wholly familiar, in Mantel's description of her childhood. My family was also poor, provincial and aspiring to respectability. I remember the determined comfortlessness, the small proprieties jealously preserved, the dogged home cooking, the bumble of kin waiting to be fed their scones and jam (in Mantel's case, cheese and ham); the energetic women in their Turkish domestic seclusion; the perfection of the Catholic/Protestant divide even when 'they' lived next door. I had also wondered at the startling whiteness of working men's inner arms, but since I am of a more secular bent than Mantel (lapsed Presbyterian versus practising Catholic) it did not occur to me, as it did to her more metaphysical mind, that they might be humans transubstantiating into vegetables. I thought they might be princesses in elaborate but sportingly defective disguise. Who else in my world could plausibly claim milk-white skin and sky-blue veins?

The richness of Mantel's descriptions also tempts us into the disreputable game of identifying 'real' images and moments in the novels. Her grandfather's brothers used to come *en masse* to visit, always without warning, because 'this is the time before telephones, or before anyone went anywhere, to be out when you called'. I remember those times too, when our suburban fortress would suddenly be overrun by unannounced hordes of kin. Mantel's great-uncles, 'in many woollen layers', their caps still on their heads and 'coughing wetly', would sit on upright chairs 'set at each end of the sideboard, symmetrical, at the back of the room, as if an opera were about to burst out in front of the fireplace', and as I laugh I think 'so that's where those Ghazzah chairs come from', and eye my own furniture arrangements queasily: what unseen guests are sitting in those empty chairs, waiting for some invisible show to begin—or, worse, already playing? Fans will also spot the childhood springs of *Fludd*. *Fludd* is Mantel's revenge on the Catholic Church: a realistic fable of a liberating Devil disguised as a priest who seduces and thus saves a healthy, good-humoured young nun from the dreary rigours of convent life. In her memoir, Mantel confesses that her knowledge of convents came from a single penetration into a dark convent interior made when her mother sent her to deliver a message to the cluster of whiskery old nuns she found at its heart. Her child's eyes had gulped down everything.

In pre-school years Mantel was small in stature but large in hopes, a cheerful, ambitious child in a family where adult arrangements were lovingly stretched to meet her flaring imagination: an Indian teepee pitched on her grandmother's floor, a great-aunt confiding her sins to her five-year-old niece in the role of priest. Mantel was a passionate consumer of stories from her pre-literate days: a reverse Ancient Mariner waylaying passing kin and requiring them to read her a chapter from 'King Arthur and the Knights of the Round Table'. (Just one. Mantel was an honourable child, jealous of her own rights, respectful of others'.)

Through those stories she came to trust in the reality of benign transformations. Had not her mother told her that she had been born with long black hair, while her hair was now fair? Might she not once have been, and therefore be destined to become, a Red Indian? While she had been born female, she was emphatically unfeminine in her vigour, audacity and taste for battle toys. She was therefore confident that when she was four she would turn into a boy, and assume either of the two destinies—Arthurian knight or Indian brave—for which she was preparing herself. Her rigorous child's logic only increased the reach of her imaginings.

A transformation did come at four, but not one of her choosing: her body thinned to spindly frailty, and a series of shattering fevers saw her long, heavy hair cut off and replaced by pale fluff. Abruptly transformed from warrior-in-waiting to pallid girl-child, she knew her destiny had been altered without her consent. Not long afterwards she was ejected from her loving home into the tedium and torment of 'school', a place of impenetrable questions from teachers ('Do you want me to hit you with this ruler?') and casual violence from students. Primary schools then were not the technicolor edens they appear to be now. Mine was the most violent society I have known. Both Mantel and I had to learn to punch to defend our dignity from the 'big boys' who saw small girl-children as their natural prey. I have a potent memory of my big brother, pillow across his middle, giving me instruction: 'At the first hint of trouble, step in close, short-arm jabs to the solar plexus right, left, right, *with* your weight behind it; step back. And if you have to go in again, keep your head down, step in and *keep punching*.' These instructions proved shockingly effective. I haven't had to hit anyone since I was eight, but it has been a useful ongoing lesson in how to deal with bullies. Mantel's grandad taught her much the same routine, although he favoured one good hard blow to the middle followed by a fast slap across the chops.

These strategies came later. At first, this tough, inventive, verbal child declined into silent weeping and unspecific illnesses, to be dubbed by a complacent doctor—the first of that ominous line of medical fools—'Little Miss Neverwell'. Mantel, already persuaded of the magical power of words, furiously resented that casual, prophetic 'naming'.

Meanwhile there was deepening malaise at home. Her mother, resentful of poverty and the stifling dictates of respectability, rebelled, moving her family (now there were two little brothers) from the contiguous kin households to an echoing house on a windy hill. There she took a male lodger first into her house, then into her bed, reducing her husband to lodger status. The child became an anxious ghost roaming the house, watching closed doors, struggling to comprehend what was happening—kept, as she bitterly remembers, literally in the dark.

When she was seven, Mantel took instruction, then the Catholic sacraments, and waited hopefully for her infusion of grace. This was a smart child. She had understood the bleak message that mere wanting would have nothing to do with it: that God's decision was arbitrary, and without appeal. Then one ordinary morning, instead of grace, something else came: a vile something 'as high as a child of two', manifesting as a vaporous movement in a patch of grass near the new house, and rousing instant terror and revulsion. 'Within the space of a thought' it invades her body, and 'grace runs away from me, runs out of my body like liquid from a corpse'. Mantel acknowledges that after this experience she was 'always more or less ashamed and afraid'.

When she was ten her parents' shell of a marriage finally cracked and her mother decamped to another city, with her lover and her children, to begin what she was determined would be a new life. Mantel never saw her father again, and contact with her beloved grandparents was intermittent. The company of two little brothers, so young at the time of the family rearrangement that they came to think the usurping stepfather was their father, could not mitigate her isolation.

Mantel marks the family rupture as ending her childhood. During those years she had learnt the high cost of other people's freedom. She also absorbed, after her infant dreams of autonomy, the helplessness of children in an adults' world. In exchange she gained a peaceful school run by intelligence-tolerant nuns, a domineering stepfather and a burden of silent, obdurate memories. Seven moderately calm years later, intelligence and a fierce will had delivered her to London and the first year of a law degree. She found the man she would love. And then the pains began.

Mantel's account of her younger self explodes sentimental notions of childhood, replacing them with a mound of bladed memories and unanswerable questions. What is childhood? Lewis Carroll's 'nest of gladness', an edenic prelude before the bread, sweat and tears of adult life? Or the dooming time when fatal dies are cast, with everything to follow sad iteration? Are children new-washed slates, waiting for the adult world to scribble and over-scribble its gnomic messages until they can decipher the minimal requirements for adulthood in their society? Mantel remarks, with uncharacteristic wanness, that her unhappy childhood was nobody's fault: that she was simply 'not suited to being a child'. I doubt that anyone is suited to being small, powerless and ignored, especially at the time when, being all character and no experience, we have to learn to survive in a world run by unpredictable and wholly disingenuous giants. I also suspect that it is only the giants who confuse childhood, that state of chronic underemployment, humiliating ignorance and total dependence on a whimsical authority, with 'happiness'.

The Mantel account suggests that we are our truest selves as infants. Then comes the bruising world, and with it the realisation that not only other people but our own bodies can fail us, that 'experience' can and will rewrite character. And yet...what most struck me, reading Mantel, was how continuous her temperament seemed, from infant to adult. She was bloodied, yes, but not broken, indeed not even much bent, by her experiences. Of course the experiences affected her. Consider her infant conviction that she was 'by nature' male. This was not the manifestation of some immutable genetic sexual predilection, but a sensible conclusion drawn from her observation. In her time and place (as in mine) women's lives were acknowledged to be dull and trivial, while men's lives were respected and even potentially glamorous. To discover that one was irremediably a girl was a body blow to aspirations towards an honourable and interesting autonomy.

Looked at from a sufficient distance, Mantel's and my life profiles seem to follow similar trajectories. Both our mothers left school for the factory at fourteen and resented it, both married and regretted it, and both mistrusted the world. Our primary schools were lawless places where apprehension first rendered us mute and incredulous, then warily aggressive. At secondary school we both learnt that literacy and a fluent tongue were better weapons than fists. We both escaped to university, suffered the isolation of prolonged illness and its consequences, and struggled to keep body and soul together by writing.

The divergences are instructive. My parents stayed together, with no hope of happiness and not much mutual liking. I used to think that was a wrong decision, were it anything so formal as a decision. Now I think it was probably right. Tolerance grew with the years, and their children grew up in a household secure to the point of dreariness. There was sport at my secondary school, none at Mantel's: nuns don't do that kind of thing. It is only now as I lose my sense of physical competence that I realise how good a companion it has been through the years, especially when I was ill and its memory kept me hopeful and ambitious. For Mantel, after all those childhood fantasies of intrepid horsemanship and swordplay, it has been a grievous and continuing deprivation. I was handed a free university education; Mantel had to go hungry for hers. For both of us there was illness and a chronic aftermath, but my medicos proved to be wise men, while Mantel's were neglectful fools. Above all, I have children. She has none.

We have also made quite different accommodations to the world. I am a child of the Enlightenment. For me, nightmares, like neighbours or nature, are there to be analysed. I believe ghosts will vaporise with steady looking. Now, having lived inside Mantel's world for a month, I feel an expansion into an unfamiliar way of seeing: a temptation to yield to the sense that we are shadow-twins, that I have lived an earlier, sunnier, antipodean version of her life—that I have somehow filched her luck. She lets me play Grandmother's Steps with a different, scary account of the world.

What ought we make of Mantel's 'ghosts'? Physiological disturbances signalling the onset of migraine? The thing that took physical possession of her child's body: was that a 'realisation' of Catholic teachings exacerbated by a child's shame at the masked improprieties within her own household? Another accidentally parallel experience helped me to understand the shame her visions caused her. When I was deeply ill I was assaulted by horribly realistic, coherent hallucinations. I told neither my family nor my doctors. I did not 'decide' not to tell. The prohibition was absolute. The necessity was, simply, there. I would have died rather than tell. Why? I think it was because I felt that secret experience marked me as an exile from, even a traitor to, the unshadowed world of the well. I had seen what they had not. I was no longer of their kind. Read from that angle, our shared dread springs from the isolating terrors of social disconformity.

Can the adult Mantel's distinctive sensibility be explained by that confluence of infant sorrows: harsh schooling; Catholic teachings (which to my secular mind looks more and more like the psychological equivalent of foot-binding); the hidden horrors of a 'respectable' marital breakup? Perhaps. But there is an archaic dimension to Mantel's sensibility, of weird forces moving under the surface of things, which makes these brisk modern explanations seem glib. I doubt that her particular spirit (and by analogy ours) can be so easily caught, pinned and classified.

Consider again that early anxiety jig or, in my interpretation, war dance: 'the preliminary working-up of courage and energy before a major exploit'. Cultures accommodate different experiences and different temperaments with different degrees of comfort. The infant Mantel thought she was, had been or would become a Plains Indian. The poignancy is that she would have made a very good Indian with her touchy sense of honour, her zeal for self-testing, even her concern for appearance—had she only been born in the right place and the right time and had she been male. Even as a female, she would have found words and a respectful audience for those moments when a piece of the world seems to liquefy and rearrange itself into wavering, supernaturally compelling phantoms. Plains Indians would have welcomed her visions as insights into the 'really real', not dismissed them as physiological derangements or symptoms of repressed guilt. They would have been a source of social power, not a disabling secret shame.

Mantel was early persuaded of the possibility of transformations, I think by her belief in the truth of words. She attaches a time to her first conviction of unworthiness: 'From about the age of four I had begun to believe I had done something wrong...there was something inside me that was beyond remedy and beyond redemption.' Was this because she had fallen ill and so botched her chance to become a boy? At seven came the experience of physical invasion by quintessential evil, partly in response to intolerable pressures, some of them theological. Nonetheless—from the evidence of the memoir I would say that her ability to see the world from a de-arranged angle—to experience 'enchantment', malign or benign—was present in her before school, before instruction in the faith, and when the alienation between her parents was still a shadow. In a more superstitious age I might have said she had been born with a caul.

To this point I have been treating *Giving Up the Ghost* as an archive of authentic experience. Mantel insists that her memories are not a clutter of foxed snapshots faded to sepia, but vivid short films playing in her head as sensuously complex as the actuality that generated them. But my local library catalogues her book as 'autobiographical fiction'. How much fabrication is there in memory honestly recalled? A. S. Byatt declared autobiography to be the most inventive form of fiction, but A. S. Byatt is a cynic. The psychologist Jerome Bruner brings us closer to a useful understanding when he asks us to reflect on the interdependence between experience and imagination displayed in a universal activity of which we are less than unaware: the work we put into 'the rough and perpetually changing draft of our autobiography that we carry in our minds'.

That recognition made, autobiography becomes for Bruner 'an extension of fiction rather than the reverse...the shape of life comes first from imagination rather than from experience'. That feels close to right. My one quarrel with Bruner concerns his suggested sequence. With Mantel, we seem to watch imagination transfiguring experience *as it happens*. Remember this was a child peculiarly sensitive to language, bewildered by the idea of lying, threatened by riddling speech, enraged by casual misrepresentation. Like the young Janet Frame, she knew that words had power ('Little Miss Neverwell') and must be treated with respect.

Consider now this one example of the dense interweaving of action and 'subject interpretation'. As a toddler, Mantel would occasionally be taken to Manchester to visit her father's grandparents, first by both parents, then, as the marriage withered, by her father alone. Once there, a large boy cousin would be prevailed upon to walk her to the park. She tells us: 'I do not remember Geoffrey's face at all, only his huge legs in flapping flannel shorts, the blunt bony bulk of his knees,' and we brace ourselves for sexual tamperings. But big, good-hearted Geoffrey did something rather worse: 'Back at the house [he] would trap me between items of furniture, sticking out one of those huge legs to prevent me toddling the way I meant to go, then when I turned back barring me with an outstretched arm, so I revolved about and about in a tearful muddle...I saw myself through his eyes, silly, frilly, too tiny to outwit or hit him, baby fist clenched in exasperation.' We have all stood by and watched toddlers teased to helpless fury. But Mantel tells us how the scene looked from the inside: 'This picture dismayed me, so far was it at odds with my own image of myself...my judgment of Geoffrey was that only the accident of my small size concealed my great superiority to him in every way. And this made it doubly galling, that I was stuck in an alley between armchairs.' (The difficulty with Mantel is that you want to give up this foolish business of reviewing, and simply go on quoting until the book is done.)

It can sometimes seem as if Mantel's life has been scripted by Mantel, pivoting as it does on a series of malign transformations of self and circumstance that might have been inflicted less than deliberately (fevers, school, the loss of her father, the medical blunders), but which damaged and continue to damage her. My suspicion is that the sinister reading was not, as it were, inscribed in the events, but inherent in the experiencing sensibility.

Consider the one doll that pre-school Mantel chose to cherish. It had been named for her dimpled schoolgirl cousin Beryl. The doll was not dimpled. It had been conjured out of 'grubby green satin, with satin stumps for hands and feet, features inked onto a round of calico for her face, and her pointed head of grubby green satin also'. Grubby satin, stumps for limbs, vestigial face, pointed head. And there it is already: the authentic Mantel shiver. As for

Mantel's first memory, when she was somewhere between twelve and eighteen months old:

> I am sitting in my pram. We are outside, in the park called Bankswood. My mother walks backwards. I hold out my arms because I don't want her to go. She says she is only going to take my picture. I don't understand why she goes backwards, back and aslant, tacking to one side. The trees overhead make a noise of urgent conversation, too quick to catch; the leaves part, the sky moves, the sun peers down at me. Away and away she goes, till she comes to a halt. She raises her arms and partly hides her face. The sky and trees rush over my head, I feel dizzied. The entire world is sound, movement. She moves towards me, speaking. The memory ends.

And there it is again: the premonitary shiver—and then the slither from the mundane into terror. The crack in the teacup that opens to swallow the world.

There is nothing confessional about this scalding memoir, and no pleas for sympathy, either. Mantel remains unreconciled to the injustices of the world, especially those visited on the ill, the poor, the over-fleshed, above all on children, whose dignity and intelligence are routinely insulted. This is not a story of the making or the deformation of a character. It seems that the mind—active, brave, rancorous—has been there from the beginning, along with the abraded sensibility and the ferocious will.

It is also the story of the making of a writer. Despite its flayed feelings, the memoir exhilarates because of its marvellously supple prose. Awareness of the authority of words might have come early. What must have come slowly is Mantel's power over words, through years of dedication, in the harshest circumstances, to the craft of writing. Mantel tells us that she wrote the memoir to lure memories of childhood from their hiding places and to exorcise them: to give up her ghosts. I think they will not go away, because they constitute her being. Instead, she has given us a gift. She has always been a good writer. This memoir demonstrates that she is now a great one.

2003

PENELOPE FITZGERALD 1916–2000

Penelope Fitzgerald began writing in 1975 when she was sixty. She went on to produce three engaging biographies, the last and best being a composite study of her father, who became editor of *Punch* when Penelope was sixteen, and his three very different brothers: one an Anglican priest, one a Roman Catholic polemicist, and one a classical scholar and cryptographer. The Knox family, with its tensions, its subdued treacheries, its perverse rapprochements, trained Fitzgerald's eye and honed her talents. At sixty-one she wrote her first novel, a detective story prompted by the Tutankhamen exhibition in London. Catholic Uncle Ronnie had written detective stories to make short clerical ends meet. Penelope wrote hers to divert her husband as he lay dying.

There followed four great novels drawn from small experiences of her own modest life rendered marvellously comic in the telling. The Knox brothers' lives and writings had been full of public clamour, charged with public import. Her writing has the quiet of the home cave. Fitzgerald was the laureate of the arbitrariness and the incorrigibility of human affections: those preferences we feel, on no clear grounds or on no grounds at all, which prove ineradicable through time. There were some villains in her books in the eyes of other characters, or even in their own. She never thought them villains. Her tranquil affections did not waver.

Then, having drawn enough from her own life, she produced three historical novels, and then a fourth, *The Blue Flower*, which brilliantly joined history and family. In a year of heavyweight American contenders—de Lillo, Roth—this delicate, old-fashioned novel took out the American National Book Critics fiction award, to loud incredulity. In that novel Fitzgerald decisively subverts an argument I had been fussing over, off and on, for years. Henry James insisted that good historical novels could be written only about events occurring within the previous fifty years: beyond that, he said, the novelist was condemned to the gruesomely false or the merely picturesque. James was putting down an unfortunate woman fool enough to send him a copy of her novel, titled (alas) *The Tory Lover*. On 5 October 1901 he replied, after some preliminary cozening ('charming touch, tact and taste…a fellow craftsman…a woman of genius and courage…') thus. The italics and the capitals are, of course, his:

> The 'historical novel' is, for me, condemned, even in cases of labour as delicate as yours, to a fatal *cheapness*, for the simple reason that the difficulty of the job is inordinate and that a mere *escamotage*, in the interest of ease, and of the abysmal public *naiveté* becomes inevitable. You may multiply the little facts that can be got from pictures and documents, relics and prints, as much as you like—the *real* thing is almost impossible to do, and in its essence the whole effect is as nought: I mean the invention, the representation of the old CONSCIOUSNESS, the soul, the sense, the horizon, the vision of individuals in whose minds half the things that make ours, that make the modern world, were non-existent. You have to *think* with your modern apparatus a man, a woman—or rather fifty—whose own thinking was

> intensely otherwise conditioned, you have to simplify back by an amazing *tour de force*—and even then it's all humbug...

Then, with the knife well planted, comes the characteristic backward step: innocent hands upraised, 'I speak in general, I needn't keep insisting, and I speak grossly, summarily, by rude and provisional signs, in order to suggest my sentiments at all.'

'Rude and provisional' perhaps, but this is well thought and better said. There are some famous exceptions to the Jamesian rule: for example, J. G. Farrell's *The Siege of Krishnapur*, a tour de force firmly set in the days of the Indian Mutiny. But perhaps imperial powers change more slowly? Perhaps they don't change at all? For nearly every other case the fifty-year rule seemed a good rule of thumb. (David Malouf's magical *An Imaginary Life* only masquerades as 'historical'.) Then Fitzgerald wrote *The Blue Flower*, and I was confounded. This is, indubitably, a great novel; it is set at the close of the eighteenth century; and it stars the youthful German poet-philosopher Fritz von Hardenburgh before he became 'Novalis'. German Romanticism, at once so florid and so prissy, must be about as far from modern sensibility as you can get.

From its first page we know we are entering the foreign country of the past. As we enter the courtyard of a mansion with two young men, 'great dingy snowfalls' of soiled linen cascade from the upper windows and balconies. This is the day of the One Great Wash of the Year. Fitzgerald's nearest literary relative is Turgenev, in the indulgent irony of the glance, the tenderness for the unheroic and the domestic—and in the lovely gratuitous detail that warms a scene into life: here the children's undergarments 'fluttered through the blue air, as though the children themselves had taken to flight'.

Another country—yet we instantly recognise the people scurrying about gathering up the linen and the two abashed young men as fellow humans. Two large, complicated and extremely talkative families are the centre of the action. This would give a merely competent writer all manner of difficulties. Fitzgerald sketches them so distinctively that we effortlessly recognise each family's ethos, each individual's characteristic tone. They are made endearingly translucent to us because Fitzgerald has none of our fashionable anxieties regarding the otherness of others: she lets us flit in and out of her characters' heads; we hear the words they speak: we are told what is in their heads as they speak, and we wonder how people manage to communicate even as well as they do. She makes her most perceptive observer-commentator a small boy gifted with perfect insubordination. With him we watch the complex dance of shifting alliances, the small mutinies, all enacted within the elastic embrace of family love. Fitzgerald understands the allure of domesticity as few writers do. And as with Turgenev, there is no sense of these lives being confined to the novel. We feel them spilling joyfully beyond the edge of the page.

The core narrative is a love story. Our budding philosopher finds himself bowled over by a merry, loud, ill-educated girl who is at ease with herself, charmed by life, and quite unprepared to pay him the deference to which his doting family has accustomed him. She holds to cheerfully simple opinions that shock him ('to decide she does not believe in the life to come. What insolence. What enormity'). He discovers her to be at once intractable, and irresistible.

These people are people, but they are not as we are. 'Novalis', the philosopher-poet recognised (rather ruefully) by his chaotic family as a genius, addresses his thirteen-year-old love as 'My Philosophy'; he discourses at formidable length on the latest salt-extracting methods, he ought to be an idealistic bore—and we do not find him ridiculous. Or no more ridiculous than do the people who cherish him, and who lovingly, patiently, admiringly listen to him. There is one plain commonsensical person planted in each of these households, what I call the 'Penelope', and they are crucial, because they give us a quiet corner to sit while the arguments and the highfalutin' talk swirl around us.

Meanwhile, physical settings and experience are evoked with magical economy. An older man and his young companion are on an expedition, conversing amiably as they go. It is early winter: November, 1794. Listen:

> As they plodded on together, drops of moisture gathered and slowly fell from their hat-brims, the ends of their noses and the hairy tips of the horses' ears which the animals turned backwards as a kind of protest against the weather. Earth and air were often indistinguishable in the autumn mist, and morning seemed to pass into afternoon without a discernible mid-day. By three o'clock the lamps were already lit in the windows.

The evocation of time and place is not the least exotic, and it is also utterly persuasive. We think: 'Of course. That is how it must have been.' What we might call 'picturesque historical details'—the village abortionist called 'the Angel-Maker', the horse not yet 'roughshod' slipping on ice—slide into the action with such lovely nonchalance it is impossible to do anything but nod: this is simply the way things were. And I am drunk with envy and admiration, because this is how historians ought to write—if they dared.

Fitzgerald knows exactly what she is doing. The novel's epigraph is a notation from Novalis himself: 'Novels arise out of the shortcomings of history.' The 'shortcomings of history' are multiple, and (after reading this novel) rather too painful to count. Above all, historians cannot hear conversations. Daily chatter is lost to us. With Fitzgerald we eavesdrop on family exchanges, as when the poet's beloved Sophie is cheerfully assessed thus by his younger brother (himself later to be smitten): 'Empty as a new jug, Fritz'. We laugh, and as we laugh we realise that these are authentic human voices we are hearing, the idioms different but the sentiments familiar; that these families are not posed for the page but fondly, furiously feuding in the ways large and loving families do. There is a great deal of love in this marvellous book, and even more of that rarer commodity, intelligent affection. (There is no sex at all. Presumably Fitzgerald believes most people knew then and now how to manage that on their own.)

In this enduring texture, larger change is delicately intimated. Novalis is a dreamer, possibly a genius, but he is also a chronic innocent. His insubordinate little brother, equally intelligent, is also very much smarter and more cynical. With him a radically different kind of thinker is in the making.

Fitzgerald is charmed by the idiosyncrasies of love, but she will not permit longeurs. She moves her characters briskly through the narrative, a briskness aided by the brevity of the chapters which are as crisp as cinematic 'takes'. We watch an exchange, we know both parties better, the story moves forward a notch—and the sense of the relentless forward movement of time is at once disturbing and entirely natural, because we know, as the protagonists do not, that time is running out, as the pages to come grow thin under our anxious fingers. We wonder what shape this story will have. What will finally happen? Only in novels, never in history, is chronic contingency briefly overcome.

And then, in an elegant manoeuvre that reminds me irresistibly of an expert skier making a dazzling, eye-baffling turn, Fitzgerald shifts her weight, adjusts her balance—and we are skimming off in a quite different direction. Novalis is no longer the hero. Laughing, shrieking Sophie, the 'empty jug' we have come, rather guiltily, to cherish precisely because of her blessed exuberance, is stricken with 'tuberculosis'. Subjected to a series of terrible operations, she suffers them with the resolution and moral grace the moonstruck Fritz had always tried, in the face of all of the evidence, to ascribe to her. (Here Fitzgerald draws on Fanny d'Ably's exquisitely horrible account to her sister of her own mastectomy, performed in 1811.)

Sophie dies two days after her fifteenth birthday. She is Sophie to the last. She does not lose her laughter. But she has become our Sophie now. We weep for her, and resent it when a back note tells us that her Fritz remarried before the year was out. But that is how life was lived—had to be lived—at the turn into the nineteenth century. Nearly every one of the children we meet in these pages will die before their thirtieth year. It is that familiarity with death—both with its prospect, and its reality—which makes this novel truly historical. These people's lives are shaped by exigencies different from ours. Curiously, and despite the dread, their world also seems more open than ours. They hope more than we do. Some of them are eager to seek the blue flower of unique destiny, while others lovingly guard the seekers against death.

Now Penelope Fitzgerald herself is dead, and for some of us darkness will be mixed with the colours of the world for a season. She was eighty-three years old, she was tough-minded, perhaps she didn't mind her dying. But I mind. Every one of her books is different, and every one of them seems to speak directly to me, to my private pleasure and enlightenment. I have been saving one of her novels, the Russian one, *In the Beginning of Spring*, like a hoarded Christmas chocolate tweaked occasionally for the joy of hearing the cellophane creak. It was a reliable something to look forward to. Now? I suppose I'll still read it. But not yet. It would make me too sad, knowing that she, a quiet presence living in another country, has quit our shared world.

2000

ANNE FRANK

Autobiographies are now acknowledged to be an unreliable form of fiction. Confessional autobiographies from the days of faith had their splendour—men and women wrestling with their darker selves under the Divine Searchlight—but in these disenchanted days we know that what we are probably watching is a mirror-dance, with every angle calculated. Yet we still hunger for intimate communication with an unguarded soul. We also know we represent ourselves most honestly in the private conversation we conduct with ourselves in our heads. The implication is that, of all forms of literature excepting possibly poetry, the diary is our most intimate, most honest, form of communication. When we talk to our diary we are talking to an intimate 'other', lightly distanced by the process of writing: an other almost but not quite ourselves.

That makes diaries—good diaries, not the 'chops for lunch' variety—one of the most engaging forms of reading there is. Our obscure but powerful hunger to know the minutiae of some other life is satisfied. We can even do it in what feels like real time. We learn our new friend's humours, fears, irritations; her responses to the weather and to different times of day. Diaries might satisfy our passion for the humdrum but they typically lack plot. It is different when the diary-story is unfolded to us against a background of great and dangerous events, when we know, as the diary-keeper does not, that this story has a beginning, a middle, and then a catastrophic end—when our knowledge of that ending is made more poignant because she who writes so engagingly is still on the edge of childhood—then a diary takes on a terrible intensity. And when the diary-keeper is a writer of perception and vitality well beyond her years, when we have a sense of a precocious talent which matures as we look at it, which we know will be brutally terminated—we have something remarkable. We have the diary of Anne Frank.

The bare events are as follows. Frank received her diary on her thirteenth birthday in June, 1942, in an Amsterdam already under German occupation. On 6 July, 1942 she and her family went into well-prepared hiding with three, later four, other Dutch Jews. Her last diary entry is dated 1 August, 1944. We know that on 4 August a car drew up, there were feet on the stairs, a pounding on a hidden door, and the Franks and the people hiding with them were taken into custody and sent by train to Westerbrook, the holding camp for Dutch Jews. On 3 September they were shipped by cattle-truck to Auschwitz. At the end of October Anne and her older sister were sent to Bergen-Belsen as part of the Nazi drive to move 'useful' prisoners deeper into a beleaguered Germany. Late in February or early in March the Frank girls succumbed to the typhus raging in the starving camp. Bergen-Belsen was liberated by British troops on 12 April, 1945.

The books under review seek to flesh out that bald narrative, and also to diagnose the fascination the Frank diary holds for us. Melissa Müller is a journalist who lives in Munich and Vienna and specialises in child-related issues; Carol Ann Lee, born in Yorkshire, confesses to an early fascination with Anne Frank (she claims to have read the diary at eight) that has intensified with the years.

Both in English and appearing in the same year, the two biographies are inevitably in competition. They also have a more formidable competitor: we now have the diary in the 'definitive edition' issued by Penguin in 1997. Why do we need biographies at all? Frank, young though she was, was a vivid writer, and a self-conscious and ambitious one. The diary might have begun life as her confidante, but even in the earliest sections we see her literary muscles begin to flex as the self-and-other analyses become more clear-sighted, the reported conversations more pointed, the humour more pungent. It is true that when, in 1944, Frank realises the possible political usefulness of her work in recording life under the Nazis, the writing loses some of its transparency, but in exchange it gains in analytic power.

The Frank diary stands as a remarkable piece of literature, independent of the tragic personal biography which was itself a part of a much larger history. We feel we come to know this cocky, sometimes infuriating girl even better than her family did: to recognise her peculiar genius, to love her more knowledgeably. We fear for her as we would for a friend. These days we are hardened to statistics, but to imagine this one particular girl terrified, brutalised, despairing, teaches us the grotesque cruelty at the heart of the Nazi ambition to rid Europe of its Jews. We are made to realise that the Nazis' destruction of Anne Frank's life and future, and the lives and futures of those millions of other irreplaceable individuals, is an inexpungeable offence against humankind.

So do we need more words beyond the diary itself? Müller's biography persuades me that we do. Müller was given unrestricted access to all the known Frank documents, including the diary's famous 'missing pages'; she tracked down and interviewed the Frank's surviving kin, friends and neighbours; her book contains an authenticating note from Miep Gies, one of the Franks' main helpers. Hers is the Authorised Version of Anne Frank's life, as proclaimed in its majestic title: *Anne Frank: The Biography*. It could therefore be saccharine, banal, a monument to sentimentality. It is none of those things. Throughout, Müller's account is marked by solid knowledge, steady intelligence, even a bracing scepticism. The context of family, friends and country is reconstructed and delicately drawn. We are brought to value these people in their affections and in their innocent preoccupation with their daily affairs. We watch the manoeuvrings of the Nazi predators, the mundane courage of the Franks' Dutch helpers, the discipline of imprisoned people who keep up their reading and their callisthenics as the slow months creep past—and as we watch we increasingly dread the denouement.

Müller's detailed account of what happened after the Franks and their friends were seized is largely new, and teaches us new, painful things. A small example: we know Anne to be physically modest, as young girls are, expecting and even demanding respectful tenderness from those around her. She was also vain about her luxuriant hair. Then we glimpse her naked, trembling, her head and pubic hair being shaved by strange male hands, and we measure more exactly another dimension of Nazi vileness.

The comparison between the two biographies is to Carol Ann Lee's detriment. (Be warned: the revelations promised in the publisher's blurb for *Roses from the Earth* are trivial.) Hers is a labour of love, and it shows. She can match neither Müller's knowledge nor her intellectual and literary poise. Assuming her readers to be ignorant of the progress of the Holocaust, she tries to sustain an awkward narrative overview, which makes her sudden plunges back to what she judges to be biographically important (Anne giving her cat a bath, childish letters to pen friends) both self-indulgent and disorienting. *Roses from the Earth* is often touching, but it is often tedious, too, while Müller's biography has won a permanent place on my bookshelf.

1999

AGAMEMNON'S KISS

Once upon a long time ago in the country we call Peru the Great Inca Atahualpa, child of the Sun, made a natural mistake: when he was handed a small untidy oblong package by an over-excited Spanish priest he took it, turned it over, shook it, smelled it, held it to his ear—and tossed it away. The natural mistake proved fatal; he and most of his people were to die for it, because the mute oblong was not only a Book but The Book, and the Spaniards, always sensitive to insult, had the guns. Clearly, books are powerful magic.

The notion that communication can occur by way of black squiggles marching across flat surfaces is, when you look at it, very odd indeed, especially when face-to-face, body-to-body communication is, as we know from sad experience, a long way short of perfect. Even instrumental exchanges with the person sitting opposite at breakfast are often more than we can manage. However we may deceive ourselves in moments of intimacy, 'the other' begins at the skin.

Our predicament of solitude is breached more often and more successfully by marks on paper than by any other form of communication. It is true that music and visual representations communicate something, and that something powerfully, but we must have words to describe what that something might be, and dissension erupts at that point. Felix Mendelssohn insisted that music is too precise to express in words, but while he may be right—he sounds right—the proposition is untestable. My own suspicion is that music is a solitary pleasure which may sometimes be successfully pursued in proximity to others. Poetry, which resembles music in that so much depends on silences, spaces and adjacencies, sets up its own obscure modalities. The miracle of communication is most reliably, if neither perfectly nor certainly, effected through prose.

Philip Roth has called 'the enigmatic interchange between a silent book and a silent reader...a unique transaction', and so it is: a transaction at once weird and secret. It is also to a degree accidental. We all know books which at one time have 'nothing to say' to us, and at another speak to our particular condition. We know also that these phrases about speaking are not so much metaphoric as descriptive of what actually seems to be going on. Rewarding reading is like being luxuriously absorbed in intimate conversation with a person not previously known, but whose words somehow interweave with the lonely interior monologue we conduct inside our heads. In real life we might encounter such a conversation once in every five, ten or twenty years, or possibly not at all. In a world of libraries and book shops it is forever at our fingertips, securely packaged into small objects like the one Atahualpa so innocently tossed away.

This uncarnal, intense-to-incandescent yet always accessible intimacy has no parallel in the social world, and once enjoyed it is impossible to live without. The appetite appears early, and seems to be stimulated by being read to. When does a child realise that the voice speaking to her out of a parental mouth is not the parent's voice but a new and other one, mysteriously liberated from its prison inside the boxy object her mother is holding in her hands? (For an unforgettable phenomenological description of what 'being read to' looks like, read Jean-Paul Sartre's *Words*, the story of his blissful childhood romance with books and his malformed affair with his social world. Sartre's description begins: 'Anne-Marie made me sit down in front of her, on my little chair; she leant over, lowered her eyelids and went to sleep. From this mask-like face issued a plaster voice...' Also consider the potential miracle contained within this parenthesis. By a few jiggles of my fingers I might well have set some unknown left or right hands jigging; or even pairs of legs walking, at times and in places I cannot know, towards some place of exchange in search of an oblong package labelled *Sartre* and *Words*. Close parenthesis.)

By whatever route we get to them, books supply the most reliable insights and the most durable relationships addicted readers have. If poetry and music help us experience emotions, instructing us how to feel happiness, unhappiness and most states between, fiction not only exercises sentiment, but expands experience without the discomfort of actually having to live it. It provides an indexed guide to life: Adultery-Anger-Angst. Its magic can make us weep for phantoms, because we taste their lives in our mouths.

Contrast these glories with the writing historians do. Most historians are loath to admit they are writers at all, much less magicians: they feel such claims to be pretentious, disreputable and subversive of any claim to their being scientists at work or (only apparently modestly) horny-handed labourers in the field of stone-hard facts. Writers they nonetheless are, and magicians, too. Consider: first they fold images of men and women out of their own and others' texts; then they re-present them on paper. They claim that these origami men and women they set walking, talking and travelling about closely resemble actual men and women who once walked and talked and travelled in some other place at some other time, or in our place here when it was different. They seek out the stories told about their subjects by friends and enemies, and sieve them for truth. They brood over diaries and laundry bills to recover the shape and spaces and textures of their days. They even try to discover the stories their people were telling themselves inside the privacy of their own heads. Surely to construct dead individuals never seen and never met with out of enigmatic artifacts and scratches on paper, to name them Lazarus and to claim a secular resurrection—surely this must be the work of magicians?

Historians insist it is not. Instead we say, with touching modesty but little insight, that all these remarkable things we do are simply what we do in the course of our ordinary work; that there is nothing the least occult about it. Our modesty is reinforced by our lack of esoteric equipment. Unlike all other practitioners in the human sciences, historians have no special language or special theories or special tools of trade: we are ourselves our only instrument. The uncomfortable corollary is that our skills are not exclusive: other people have them, other people use them. We depend on patient reading, careful judgment, and the cultivation of the kind of imaginative openness Keats called 'negative capability', which is an odd kind of competence to claim as 'professional'. And that is all we have.

It is our central reliance on the written word that distinguishes us from our nearest academic neighbours. Pre-historians discover what they can about people of the past largely from their material traces, because their people neglected to accompany those traces with written commentaries. I have before me a book called *The Bog People*, written by an archaeologist called Professor Glob, irresistible conjunction. There I can actually examine the Tollund Man, twenty thousand years old, as he looked when he was dug out of a Danish peat bog on a May evening in 1950. I can peer at his wrinkles, brood over his firm-shut eyelids, his soft-shut, slightly pouting mouth. He's a bit brown, but otherwise he looks much as he would have looked before he was surprised by death. Although he probably was not too surprised, because he was sacrificed and we can assume some ritual foreplay. The leather thong that killed him is still tight around his neck. He doesn't look throttled, so they must have jerked hard enough to kill him outright. He doesn't even look dead. He looks as if he were sleeping, and dreaming an absorbing, slightly vexing dream. Apart from the thong around his throat he wears a finely stitched pointed leather cap which echoes and exaggerates the curve of his fine curved nose and a narrow hide belt. Otherwise he is naked. But he doesn't look naked. He looks fully dressed in the folds of his own loose skin.

I can examine the photographs of the Tollund Man. I could go and look at him in his glass case in the Silkeborg Museum in Central Jutland, if I had the inclination and the price of the fare. Professor Glob can also tell me a surprising number of things about him, including what he ate for his last meal—he was killed several hours after he had eaten, but scientists have been able to analyse the residues in the stomach and intestines. I could, if I chose, cook that meal, an unappetising gruel of mashed seeds, and taste on my tongue what the Tollund Man last tasted on his. The exercise has in fact been carried out: the food was ground, cooked and publicly consumed before an awed audience by a team of intrepid anthropologists. They said it tasted horrible.

Now meet 'the Man in the Ice', three thousand years older than the bog man and not pickled in peat but snap-frozen in a glacier. He had been a tough, experienced hiker, well fitted out with his axe and belt-pouch, dagger and scabbard, along with a bone awl for running repairs and dried meat and tinder stowed in his backpack, but in the end the cold beat him. 'Otzi', his finders called him.

But even as I look at him I know I do not know Otzi, and I do not know the Tollund man. I cannot have any sort of conversation with them because I have access only to their bodies, not to their minds. Compare this situation with the respectful, affectionate intimacy I have with Michel Eyquem, Seigneur de Montaigne, a mere four hundred and fifty years dead but whose physical presence is at this moment presumably severely attenuated. I do not know what he ate for his last or, indeed, for any breakfast, but I know some of his thoughts because he wrote them down and I have read them. I had begun to read them in that luxurious mood of piety lace-edged with boredom with which we read the lesser classics when I came upon a thought he had had about his cat: 'When I play with my cat, who knows whether I play with her, or she plays with me?' That lovely glint of self-irony, and the Seigneur de Montaigne was revealed as a potential friend. Words had overleapt gender, class and nation, translation, death and time: another casual miracle effected by literacy.

As with most miracles, there is an element of self-deception here. My new friend is garrulous. He seems eager to tell me everything. However, as I close the book I realise I know almost nothing about the landscape he inhabited, actual and mental, and I do not know his social world. It is like the dooming doubt you have after visiting a well-loved friend in a nursing home. She seems so much herself that it is only later, when you have left her propped in her chair on the verandah and walked down the drive and started the car, that you wonder how she really is: where and how she is finding her life.

A final example of the limits of this very peculiar relationship. John Donne has always demanded intimacy, most directly through the tough allure of his love poetry, most potently through the intellectual athleticism of his religious verse. My own best conversation with Donne—a conversation more intense and more sustained than any conversation held with any living person during the same period—took place recently and in hospital, as I read the series of linked meditations he named 'Devotions upon Emergent Occasions'. They represent his reflections on his long servitude to a 'pestilentiall fever', very nearly fatal, which beset him in 1623. He compares his rebirth from illness to earlier births: 'One, Naturall, when I came into the World; One, Supernatural, when I entered into the Ministery; and now a preter-natural Birth, in returning to life, from this Sicknes.' Some fractions of the meditations can read like a preacherly pot-boiler (the work was dedicated, with a most elaborate flourish, to the man who would become Charles the First within the year) but most of them spoke directly to me, because they seemed in my drug-excited, debilitated state eerily apposite to my own less orderly, less meditative and very much less intelligent progress through and emergence from the Valley of the Shadow.

With one swipe of its paw the disease had flipped the Dean of St Paul's from the lordly vertical to the abject horizontal. It sliced away a whole existential dimension: the meditations are haunted by the image of the invalid as a two-dimensional man, flat as a map, cruelly abstracted, reduced to mere schema. The map metaphor was not new. His love poetry, written long ago, before his wife died, before he became the eminent, lonely Dean of St Paul's, throbbed with metaphors of the bed as map, of woman as enticing archipelago, of himself, jubilantly erect, as enraptured explorer and about-to-be conqueror. Now he is mere territory explored by his physicians' probing fingers, and his physicians explore only through duty, not love. He counts and recounts his single blessing: at least he is well tended, while others lie in mud. But for all their probings and their talk the physicians are useless. They cannot even name the disease, much less cure it. He knows his isolation is prudent, and experiences it as shunning: he is excommunicated from the company of men. Extravagant metaphors pullulate: his weakness is fetters, his sickbed a prison, his sickbed a grave: 'Here I am my owne Ghost.' To be seriously ill is to be paranoid. Donne imagines his once-docile body and all its parts as a murderous conspiracy against him: 'Murmurings, murmurings in their hearts, secret disobediences, secret repugnances...[while] the pulse, the urine, the sweat, have all sworn to say nothing...'

He is also ferociously bored. Time stretches unendurably; his only company is his fractious, fretful mind. Being Donne, his thoughts are huge—'born Gyants', they 'doe not onely bestride all the Sea, and land, but span the Sunn and Firmament at once'—but for all their reach they offer only a more comprehensive depression. He decides it is not freakish sickness but existence itself that constitutes the human tragedy: 'Death is in an olde mans dore, he appeares, and tells him so, and death is at a young mans backe, and saies nothing. Age is a sicknesse, and Youth an ambush.' Then as now, illness makes you sorry for yourself ('Man, who of himselfe is but dust, and coagulated and kneaded into earth, by tears...') and querulous ('How deare and how often a rent doth man pay for this [poor] farme!').

Flat as a tack in my hospital bed, my once-amenable body an every-man's-land of wire and rubber tubing, my once-expansive self reduced to two swivelling eyeballs bisected by a white cotton horizon, I took much comfort from Donne. He knew exactly what I was going through. But did I really comprehend the texture of his suffering? Through all this elongated, empty time he has been lapped by the voices of the bells of the church tower next to his dwelling as they tolled the deaths of neighbours. During the sixteenth meditation, he listens. By the seventeenth, he is famously reflecting upon the sound: 'Now, this Bell tolling softly for another, saies to me, "Thou must die..."' and so, magnificently, on to 'No man is an Island, intire of it selfe...' Listening in my turn, I add (apologetically; surely Donne of all men valued women?) 'nor no woman neither', stumbling on the negatives, and agree. We all have felt the iron blade of death beneath the velvet of love, the fustian of habit. Then in a superb cadence he lures us to vault with him to the uplands of altruism: 'Any man's death diminishes me; For I am involved in mankind.' But we—remembering Rwanda, Bosnia, Nigeria, remembering Guatemala, remembering Palestine—falter. We adjust our spectacles: surely to say this is to leap from the 'undeniably is' to the 'ideally ought'? And in any case (sitting down on the grass) surely it is not true? Indeed we do 'send to know'—photo-journalists, political observers, even occasional peace-keepers or seekers or breakers—but surely we are essentially observers, not-quite-innocent bystanders? The bell certainly does not toll for us—or at least not yet.

The conversation proceeds, but haltingly now, because for all its comforts and coincident particularities, and for all my pleasure in it, I have to acknowledge that I am not a partner in it at all, because I do not share its central understanding. There has been a silent Other present throughout this conversation. Donne here, as everywhere and always, is in contention with an unseen, often aloof but invincibly present deity. Every word he writes, including those words that might seem to me to speak only of human love, are contexted within that lacerated, anxious faith. If I want to hear and to understand him better, I will not do it by reading more Donne. I will need to do some serious reading in English Religious Thinking in the Early Seventeenth Century. I will need to do some history.

This could seem a dreary divagation, about as attractive as a stint of ditch-digging after a golden afternoon lounging in a cherry orchard. On the contrary. The search will be absorbing because I will be in pursuit of a complex, eminently real man, and because I know that the more history I do, the more nuanced, intimate and actual my continuing conversation with Donne will become.

Delights attend the doing of history—delights I see the more clearly for being for the moment exiled from them. There is great luxury in attending to the papery whispers from the past rather than the boom and babble of the present. I can listen to those dead people and think about them steadily, because I don't have to do anything about them. I don't have to rebuke them, reason with them, encourage them or fight them; I don't have to deal with them. All I have to do is to listen to them. I therefore listen with an intentness and an openness I give to almost nothing else.

There is also a suspension—not a denial, but a temporary suspension—of moral and juridical principles. Our first reading of historical texts mimics the moral irresponsibility with which we read fiction. Having been introduced to Humbert by his divine maker Nabokov, I am ready to be instructed by him. Once instructed, this respectable matron and incorrigible heterosexual who detests the misuse of power is able to scan a tumble of late primary-school girl-children with something of the eye of a nymphet-fancier. Ardent listening temporarily suspends judgment. But if I want to write about listening to real historical subjects, morality intrudes. I am entering a contract with both subject and potential reader to report precisely what it is that the voices are saying—their inflexions, intonation, emphases and, if I can manage it—if my ear is fine enough—their casual or ominous or thunderous silences. I have, after all, chosen to re-present them. They have not chosen me.

Is it necessary, then, to like them? No. Is it desirable to trust what they are saying? On the contrary: it is essential to acknowledge that one's subjects had the wit to deceive. Above all, we must accord them the respect of recognising them to be ultimately mysterious, as all humans are. It is essential to be curious about one's subjects from the beginning of the inquiry, and to remain so beyond the end—as in any dynamic human relationship. Thumbnail sketches might do for people on the periphery of our lives ('Mrs Briggs is an old cow'), but not for those, living or dead, who have become implicated in our lives. 'In reality' we are endlessly negotiating revelations about other people ('you did *that*?') and about ourselves ('*I* did that?'). Why should it be any different with the dead?

There is an early indicator of natural talent among history

students. They are the people who are puzzled about what people might mean by this or that act or this or that statement. Others are not the least curious because they think they already know. There is nothing to be done with such people. But the curious ones will go on being attentive to the mysteriousness of the apparently ordinary, and will continue to reap the benefits. And the benefits are inexhaustible, because history is the discipline that best teaches the individual how to assess the possibilities and the limitations of particular human situations, and the possibilities and limitations of the human will. We are all, men and women alike, subject to the restrictions and coercions of the social world. The trick is to recognise which restrictions we want to sustain, which to evade and which to subvert, and to decide what we will do by calculating the likely costs.

Those are the profits of History. But History has its magic, too, which for me, because I have occasionally experienced it, is more astonishing and more thrilling than the mighty magic of fiction. Of course it does not always feel like magic, but for the practitioner what magic does? The daily fare of history is finding out how little you can find out, and also what you are up against—including, of course, yourself. Nonetheless...as a child I used to tickle trout, an illicit but enthralling activity. You feel along rock ledges and submerged boulders until your fingertips touch a living, quivering, electric something, a something holding against the current. You creep your fingers gently along its length, slowly, slowly, until you have mapped it with your blind tentacles. Then you drive thumb and index finger hard into the gills, toss it onto the bank—and you have your trout.

Those first moments of tactile, sensuous encounter are unforgettable—the blind exploration, the tentative mental construction of an actual but concealed world, the excitement of obscure but vivid life under your fingertips. Like the moment of touching the trout, the moment when you think you touch some other previously inaccessible minds, some different way of conceiving the world; as you gently,

gently test to see if the shape is indeed as you think it may be—that is for me the authentic, incomparable magic of History.

The moment of magic might seem trivial to the reader. One example only: puzzling over an Aztec ritual I came upon the list of the small creatures young boys were required to catch and present to the Old Fire God in his great annual ceremony. It was an odd collection, and I worried over it for days. What taken-for-granted Aztec category made these creatures, and only these creatures, acceptable offerings? The list was not fully enumerated; there were implied 'etcetera'; what might they have been? The listed creatures inhabited air, earth, or water. None had fur, none could run. While some, like dragonfly larvae, presumably lay about waiting for collection, others were elusive, requiring quickness of eye and hand to catch. What common-sense Aztec category could possibly unite them all? And then I saw it. Their habitat was, broadly speaking, amphibian. These were the despised creatures that had sustained the Aztecs and the Old God of the Fire and the Hearth in their own historic 'youth', when they were despised refugees eking out a miserable existence in a marshy desolation. In time they would raise their glorious lake-borne city of Tenochtitlan out of those marshes, but in the days of their humiliation they did not dare compete with the flesh-fish-and-fowl hunters of the dominant resident tribes. This poor fare, lovingly collected by boy-hunters in yearly tribute to their oldest god, was therefore a 're-collection' in a double sense.

There are many such moments of near-miraculous contact with a different and once-actual world, of sensing a different mode of existence, in the course of 'doing history': when suddenly a hidden world opens, astonishing as a flower.

Excavating at Mycenae towards the end of the last century, the businessman-turned-archaeologist Heinrich Schliemann uncovered five graves close by the great Lion Gate. The graves contained skeletons, along with weapons and gold. In one grave lay five skeletons, every one of them masked with gold. Once exposed to the air the bone crumbled into dust, but the masks still glowed. That night Schliemann wrote in his diary: 'Today I kissed the lips of Agamemnon.'

As it happened, neither the mask nor the grave was Agamemnon's nor the place Agamemnon's city, and Schliemann's mouth had met metal, not flesh. The warmth he had felt against his lips was stolen from his own. To feel the kiss of Agamemnon requires the communication of thoughts, and thoughts are borne not by enigmatic objects, but, however precariously, by words. Agamemnon reserves his kiss for we happy breed who practise the magical arts of History.

1998

Big Louis
London Review of Books, July 2001

Backstage at the Republic of Letters
The Australian Academy of the Humanities Annual Lecture, November 2003

The Gecko in the Machine
Australian Book Review, November 2004

At the Beach
Bulletin, Christmas 2004

Breaking the Mirror
Australasian Journal of Psychotherapy, 2002 (vol. 21, no. 2)

Hobyahs!
Age, 2003

About Bones
The Penguin Book of Death, 1997

Postcard from Townsville
Australian's Review of Books, 2000

Fellow Sufferers
Australian Humanities Review, October 1996

Norman Mailer Meets Jack Ruby
HEAT 7 (first series), 1998

Bernhard Schlink's *The Reader*
The Australian's Review of Books, September 1998

Plenty Humbug
Australian Quarterly Essay Lecture: Acknowledging Difference: Public Intellectuals and Aboriginal Australia, May 2004

Dispatches from the History Wars
Australian Financial Review, October 2003

Building Treblinka
HEAT 14 (first series), 2000

Secret Meetings, Secret Lives
Australian Book Review, December 1997

The Crack in the Teacup: Reading Hilary Mantel
Australian Book Review, November 2003

Penelope Fitzgerald 1916–2000
Best Australian Essays, 2000

Anne Frank
Sydney Morning Herald, July 1999

Agamemnon's Kiss
Best Australian Essays, 1998